D1032172

George Eliot's Creative Conflict

George Eliot's Creative Conflict
The Other Side of Silence

LAURA COMER EMERY

University of California Press
Berkeley . Los Angeles . London

Univeristy of California Press
Berkeley and Los Angeles, California

University of California Press, Ltd.
London, England

ISBN 0-520-02979-8
Library of Congress Catalog Card Number: 75-3768
Printed in the United States of America

Contents

Introduction

That element of tragedy which lies in the very fact of frequency, has not yet wrought itself into the coarse emotion of mankind; and perhaps our frames could hardly bear much of it. If we had a keen vision and feeling of all ordinary human life, it would be like hearing the grass grow and the squirrel's heart beat, and we should die of that roar which lies on the other side of silence.

Middlemarch

If we still read George Eliot today, a century after these words were written, it is because her creations bring us closer to "a keen vision and feeling of all ordinary human life." In her best novels we are confronted with ourselves. And this happens only because in writing them, George Eliot confronted herself: she approached "the roar which lies on the other side of silence"—the hidden patterns of her own unconscious mind.

I studied the unconscious elements in the five middle novels for a long time before I realized that the author was indeed confronting herself. At the beginning of my work I could see basic similarities in the fantasy content of *The Mill on the Floss, Silas Marner, Romola, Felix Holt,* and *Middlemarch,* and my aim was to relate the underlying fantasy in each work to the defensive handling of it. I expected the varying degrees of success and failure among these works to be directly related to the author's defensive handling of the fantasies. And to a limited extent this proved to be the case. It was possible to establish that the flood-death ending of *The Mill on the Floss* is an inadequately controlled expression of feared and largely unconscious impulses, and that the lack of control mars the novel. It was also possible to demonstrate the relationship between over-defensiveness and the failure of *Romola*. But treating the other three novels solely in these terms became somewhat mechanical. I felt myself producing what Frederick Crews aptly labels "anaesthetic criticism," a kind of analysis that "cheerfully catalogs the unconscious tricks we play on ourselves and equates literary power with a judicious recipe of wishes and tactics, introjection and intellection."[1] As I struggled with George Eliot's treatment of Dorothea in *Middlemarch* I finally realized that the development I wanted to describe could not be expressed in terms of fantasy and defense alone.

In strictly Freudian terms, "meaning" in literature seems to be necessarily confined to what Norman Holland has called a defensive or "ego-syntonic transformation of the unacceptable fantasy content."[2] The meaning of George Eliot's novels, for me, comes from my own participation in the author's painful process of self-confrontation, psychic readjustment, and growth. This kind of meaning is clearly beyond the scope of literary meaning as defense. It involves much more than

[1] "Anaesthetic Criticism," in *Psychoanalysis and Literary Process*, ed. Frederick Crews (Cambridge, Mass., 1970), p. 19.
[2] *The Dynamics of Literary Response* (New York, 1968), pp. 180-81.

a change in defensive tactics. And it demands a more positive view of the creative process than strictly Freudian concepts allow.

It is not one of my aims, here, to construct a neo-Freudian aesthetic or a new model for adapting psychoanalytic insights to the ends of literary criticism. But in order to be true to my own experience I must point out that, while I am more convinced than ever of the value of applying Freudian concepts to the understanding of literature, I see a need to keep testing them and searching for better ways to apply them. And that search will, it seems, require as intensive a study of the creative process as Freud's of neurosis.[3]

In the following chapters I attempt to integrate my perception of George Eliot's inner conflict and increasing self-awareness with the analysis of fantasy and defense. Thus the flood-death ending of *The Mill on the Floss* is presented not only as expressive—a culmination of the author's unconscious impulses traced through the novel, but also as generative—a symbolic articulation of self which disrupts the author's psychic equilibrium. As such the inadequately controlled fantasy in *The Mill on the Floss* can be seen as influencing the author's subsequent works. *Romola*, which George Eliot intended as her next novel, is weighed down by intensified counter-instinctual demands. But *Silas Marner*,

[3] There are already significant beginnings. Anthony Storr in *The Dynamics of Creation* (New York, 1972) brings together a variety of evidence indicating that the objectification of fantasy in art yields not only pleasure but a "closer grip upon reality" (p. 140). His book came to my attention only after my own work was essentially finished, and I have not attempted to incorporate his findings here. I do wish to point out, however, that there is increasing support for a more positive view of art within a basically Freudian framework.

emerging while those demands were focused on *Romola* and blocking its creation, expresses a new awareness of the author's primitive self. *Felix Holt* reflects and explores both sides of the author's conflicting demands with a guardedness that often turns to evasion. But in *Middlemarch* these tentative and fragmentary self-explorations find their "complete embodiment."[4]

Middlemarch reflects a mind that has regained equilibrium and integration at a new level. It expresses the same fantasies as the preceding novels, controlled more perfectly. But its excellence is not merely a matter of control. *The Mill on the Floss*, though imperfectly controlled, is great in the personal intensity which belongs to the first full expression of needs and suffering we all share. *Middlemarch* is the culmination of a decade of creative conflict made possible by that first full expression. Its greatness is not one of personal intensity but lies in the breadth and balance of vision belonging to self-knowledge and self-acceptance.

[4] See p. 143 below.

One

The Mill on the Floss

The Mill on the Floss is Maggie's story, and its focus on one central character is unique among George Eliot's multi-centered novels. It is also the closest thing to autobiography ever written by her. Maggie is not only "essentially identical with the young Mary Ann Evans,"[1] as F. R. Leavis puts it; she is a self which the author at the age of forty felt compelled to confront.

I hope to show, in this interpretation of *The Mill on the Floss* and subsequent chapters, that through the creation of Maggie, George Eliot does indeed begin to confront herself and recognize (not altogether consciously) the nature and strength of the forces at war within her. I do not accept Leavis' criterion of maturity, by which he finds the author lacking in her understanding of Maggie,[2] yet neither will I try to refute him by attempting to prove that the author does have a mature grasp of her heroine. On the contrary, my intention is to show that George Eliot's creation of Maggie is the

[1] *The Great Tradition* (New York, 1964), p. 39.
[2] Ibid., pp. 42-43, 46.

beginning of a process that might be called maturing—a
process which can begin only when the tyranny of the
moral code which Leavis calls "mature intelligence" is
somehow undermined.

I find myself in the position of agreeing with Leavis
that George Eliot does not stand safely outside Maggie's
immaturity, and that she does not understand it—at
least not in the last two books of the novel. Leavis
seems to deplore the author's lack of distance; I do not.
The ending of the novel is more than just a glorious
self-deception for George Eliot and her readers. It is an
explosive expression of conflicting needs, as powerful
as a primal scream but more complex. It mars the novel
as a thing in itself because it impairs the reader's sense
of security, and thus his ability to experience with
Maggie. But the death of Maggie, for whom there is no
other release from the conflict between intense desires,
equally intense fears, and a rigid conscience, is a true
beginning for George Eliot. If her mature intelligence
had maintained control of *The Mill on the Floss,* she might
have written a different novel with a less troubling
ending. But once her mature intelligence has been
swept aside long enough for Maggie's irresolvable conflict to find its end in death, the author is faced with a
new reality which demands painful readjustments and
results in further maturing—further extension of her
self-awareness and sense of truth.

There is abundant evidence that for nearly ten years
after the completion of *The Mill on the Floss* George Eliot
was undergoing "a period of painful readjustment and
recuperation."[3] According to Miriam Allott the ill-

---

[3] Miriam Allott, "George Eliot in the 1860's," *Victorian Studies* 5
(December 1961): 98-99.

health, emotional depressions, and lack of creative vitality that characterize the novelist's state of mind and work in the 1860s are symptomatic not of any significant change in her sceptical humanist doctrines, but of a deepening of her "emotional and imaginative apprehension of them." I recognize the validity of this view, and readily concede that George Eliot was "facing for the first time the more sombre implications of her own doctrines." But the word "doctrines" is inadequate. The evidence of struggle and despair marshaled by Miriam Allott does not preclude the possibility, but in fact implies it, that on a deeper level the novelist was facing *herself* for the first time, and that self as expressed in Maggie had more somber implications for her than any doctrine.

What does this mean for our understanding and evaluation of the novels? To me it means that the expression of self and of despair accomplished in the creation and destruction of Maggie, although it mars *The Mill on the Floss* and seems to inhibit George Eliot's creativity in *Romola* and *Felix Holt,* is a painful confrontation with which the earnest, truth-seeking, creative woman struggles until she comes to a new knowledge and acceptance of herself—a new vision which ultimately gives her creative imagination greater vitality than ever before, so that the painful process of growth and adjustment culminates in the writing of *Middlemarch,* a novel which is mature in the highest sense of being able to "extend our sense of truth"[4] rather than simply to satisfy our commonly accepted values and moral distinctions.

[4] Frederick Crews, "Anaesthetic Criticism," in *Psychoanalysis and Literary Process,* ed. Frederick Crews, (Cambridge, Mass., 1970), p. 21.

The psychoanalytic interpretations which follow will give substance to the unsupported assertions I have been making. They concentrate more on the latent content of the novels than on the manifest content, but in every case the object of interpretation is the same—to show how the mind of the author is struggling to find alternatives to death and despair by allowing the characters who succeed Maggie as extensions of the author's psyche to put some limits on the tyranny of conscience, to find some outlets for libidinal needs, and thus to find ways of reconciling the opposing forces of id and superego.

I will begin by exploring the relationship between the id impulses and superego demands expressed through Maggie, and the reader is asked to remember that my analysis ultimately refers to a fantasy originating in the unconscious needs of Maggie's creator, George Eliot. The main task of this chapter is to scrutinize the makeup of and the changes in Maggie, the character whose inability to reconcile competing claims leads to death. Part I relates Maggie's wished-for death to oral needs; Part II relates the destructive flood and the moral victory over Tom to anal-sadistic needs and traces both oral and anal needs to revived Oedipal conflict; Part III shows how these regressive needs affect Maggie's relationship to Stephen Guest, and then turns to a consideration of George Eliot's difficulties in managing the wish-fulfilling ending.

I

The embrace of brother and sister as they drown at the end of *The Mill on the Floss* points very clearly to an Oedipal fantasy which can be traced as an important structural element in the novel. David Smith's psychoanalytic interpretation uses the controversial flood-death ending to illuminate earlier portions of the novel, and thus to demonstrate its "thematic unity."[5]

But the tracing of the incest theme leaves unanswered crucial questions about the significance of Maggie's death and about the nature of her relationship to Tom. The flood-death ending itself is no more a simple Oedipal wish-fulfillment than it is a mere reunion of a brother and sister. When Maggie Tulliver finds herself in a boat on the flooding river, she is about to receive, under the guise of her conscious wish to rescue Tom, satisfaction of *several* repressed wishes. The reunion with Tom fulfills oral and Oedipal wishes. It is also a complex victory composed of a brief rescue, which proves Maggie's superiority over a rival sibling, followed by destruction satisfying anal rage. At the same time Maggie's death satisfies a self-destructive impulse and fulfills a desire

[5] " 'In their death they were not divided': The Form of Illicit Passion in *The Mill on the Floss,*" *Literature and Psychology* 15, iii (1965): 146. Smith's interpretation establishes that the ending of the novel is psychologically congruent with the rest of the novel. I don't agree with him, however, that the psychological unity is equal to artistic coherence. A more comprehensive examination of the latent content and its relation to defensive representation enables us to see not only why the ending is a necessary culmination, but also why it is to some extent artistically flawed. See also Bernard J. Paris, "The Inner Conflicts of Maggie Tulliver: A Horneyan Analysis," *Centennial Review* 13 (Spring 1969): 166-99.

to return to the warmth and oneness of the womb and thus to an un-individuated, pre-sexual past.

To justify this summary statement, let me begin by exploring Maggie's most regressive wish—to return to the womb. This wish, like the Oedipal wish, can be traced as one of the structural elements which unifies the novel. Maggie's death by drowning may seem like a contradiction of her wish for an "intense and varied life,"[6] but both belong to the oral need that dominates her "hungry nature" (VI, iii). Her hunger throughout is an expression of George Eliot's desire for lost oneness, the blissful unity of mother and infant which produces the oceanic feeling of primary narcissism.

Throughout the novel Maggie strives to deal with her overwhelming need—to satisfy it through the love and approval of a series of love objects, to deny it through asceticism and adherence to duty. The aim of both approaches is to obliterate the painful separation between the self and some greater being and thus to recapture the lost unity and feeling of well-being. But when Maggie's striving is ultimately frustrated, partly by unaccommodating reality and partly by her own conflicting demands, her unsatisfied longing becomes a wish for death, and she is engulfed by the flooding river as she has longed to be engulfed by the love of a greater being.

From the beginning of the story Tom is the primary object through whom Maggie seeks to gratify her oral need for love and approval and for oneness. Their re-union during the flood seems to realize Maggie's hope

---

[6] George Eliot, *The Mill on the Floss,* ed. Gordon S. Haight, Riverside Edition (Boston, 1961), bk. VI, chap. ii. Subsequent references are to this edition.

that "great calamity" will prove them "one with each other in primitive mortal needs" (VII, v). Their final embrace gets this brief comment: "brother and sister had gone down in an embrace never to be parted: living through again in one supreme moment the days when they had clasped their little hands in love, and roamed the daisied fields together" (VII, v). But the emphasis on childhood unity and "daisied fields," however harmonious with Maggie's hopes, looks like an evasion. It comes from the author of the epitaph, "In their death they were not divided," and distracts attention from the key word—"death."

Maggie's hope for reunion with Tom recapitulates the wishful conclusion of the dream in which her impulse toward Tom overturned the boat and, as she began to sink, she suddenly seemed to "awake and find she was a child again in the parlour at evening twilight, and Tom was not really angry" (VI, xiv). This dream and the final embrace of Maggie and Tom are essential aspects of a fantasy which readers must be able to share in order to experience the full power of the novel. But that sharing depends upon the author's ability to maintain the sense of "reality" she has created.

Before we look further at the author's relationship to the wish-fulfilling ending, let us examine the relationship of Tom to Maggie's regressive needs. The childhood scenes at the beginning of the novel are not records of blissful union. Maggie's actual moments of feeling at one with Tom are few and extremely brief. She dreams of capturing such moments and making them last, but her dreams are far removed from the reality of her relationship with Tom. If Oedipal desire alone were the basis for Maggie's persistent attach-

ment, there would be no way to account for the substi-
tution of such a difficult brother for Maggie's loving
father. But Maggie's love is complex. We are expected
to sympathize wholeheartedly with her whenever her
extreme love for Tom is met with hardness. At the
same time, a substantial series of scenes and images
suggests that Maggie's love is above all a *hunger for love*,
an expression of oral need. This becomes apparent
through a pattern of interactions with Tom that is
repeated numerous times in the novel and finally in the
ending. It is a pattern of unintentional offense by
Maggie,[7] unfair punishment by Tom, and eventual forgiveness and reunion through Maggie's pleading.

The final stage of the pattern, being forgiven and
loved again, is the goal revealing Maggie's hunger for
love. Thus, after her confession to Tom about his dead
rabbits (that she has forgotten to feed) and Tom's cruel
response ("I don't love you"), Maggie's "wretched pleasure" in condemning Tom's cruelty soon gives way to
the "need of being loved, the strongest need in poor
Maggie's nature" (I, v). Tom forgets his intention to
punish her as she clings to him, begging for his love,
and he kisses her, saying "Don't cry, then, Magsie—
here, eat a bit o' cake." The love and the cake are closely
related, for the child who loses self-esteem when he
loses love is but a shade more developed than the infant
whose feeling of well-being depends upon food.

The incident of the jam-puffs points up even more
clearly the relationship of love and food. Maggie chooses the lesser half of the sweet not out of love for Tom,
but because she wants Tom's approval even more than

---

[7] I will discuss the anal aspects of this pattern in Part II of this
chapter.

she wants food: "I fear she cared less that Tom should enjoy the utmost possible amount of puff, than that he should be pleased with her for giving him the best bit" (I, vi).[8] Her pleasure in eating, before she is aware of Tom's disapproval, approaches the oceanic feeling: "Maggie didn't know Tom was looking at her; she was seesawing on the elder bough, lost to almost everything but a vague sense of jam and idleness." Her utter passivity is a state in which no outside object exists.

Tom's denouncement of Maggie as "greedy" after she has eaten the jam-puff in submission to his rigidly fair procedure seems unjust; but it is possible that Tom's response may come from an unconscious awareness of the greediness for love that underlies Maggie's apparent generosity.

Maggie's happy day of fishing with Tom at the round pool gives us a closer look at her idea of bliss. Maggie is completely passive: Tom opens the basket, prepares the tackle, throws out the line, puts the rod in her hands, and tells her when she has a bite; Maggie looks "dreamily at the glassy water" and listens to "dreamy silences" and the gentle sounds of the water. She cares nothing about fishing or about who catches the biggest fish, but only about the chance to participate in Tom's superiority and have his approval.

This is really the only happy moment they have together. The setting is symbolic. The round pool is a perfect womb: "that wonderful pool, which the floods had made a long while ago: no one knew how deep it

[8] It should be noted that it is the narrator who points out the predominance of Maggie's need for love over her concern for Tom. The narrator becomes less loquacious and much less objective in the last books of the novel.

was; and it was mysterious, too, that it should be almost a perfect round, framed in with willows and tall reeds, so that the water was only to be seen when you got close to the brink" (I, v). Thus Maggie's one experience of unity with Tom seems to be linked with an unconscious memory of the womb, and we begin to see that Tom is, at one level, a mother substitute.

The round pool relates back to other retreats—less perfect retreats because of the absence of Tom. In the great attic, Maggie submerges herself in emotion: her sobbing "expelled every other form of consciousness— even the memory of the grievance that had caused it" (I, iv). And in "the great spaces of the mill" she feels herself part of "an uncontrollable force":

The resolute din, the unresting motion of the great stones, giving her a dim delicious awe as at the presence of an uncon- trollable force—the meal forever pouring, pouring—the fine white powder softening all surfaces, and making the very spider-nets look like faery lace-work—the sweet pure scent of the meal—all helped to make Maggie feel that the mill was a little world apart from her outside everyday life. (I, iv)

In both retreats the self and the outside world are obliterated and something close to the oceanic feeling is achieved.[9]

For a child, the longing to recapture the oceanic feeling

[9] The narrator occasionally refers to Maggie's tendency to day- dream or have "fits of absence" (VI, xiii) in a sympathetic way, implying objectivity, but his introductory reverie in "Outside Dorlcote Mill" indicates his participation in Maggie's love of passive oblivion. Like Maggie he loves the "dreamy deafness" created by the "booming of the mill" and the "rush of the water" which combine to form "a curtain of sound, shutting one out from the world beyond" (I, i). Maggie by the round pool is content to look down at the glassy water, but the narrator is "in love with moistness" and envies "the white ducks that are dipping their heads far into the water." He is projected into the water as he describes the "impetuous embrace" with which the "loving tide"

is an aspect of his normal narcissism. But Maggie's longing is not outgrown with the passing of childhood. The early books of the novel connect Maggie's continuing narcissistic need to oral frustration and rejection by her mother. As Bernard Paris points out:

It is primarily through her mother that the negative attitudes of her culture towards her kind of person are transmitted to Maggie. Mrs. Tulliver gets her sense of worth and of orientation in the world through her conformity to the ways and values of the Dodson clan. Maggie's deviations from the Dodson ideal fill her with anxiety, and she is deeply ashamed of her daughter. Mrs. Tulliver's displeasure manifests itself in an "habitual deprecation" of Maggie, and her daughter's self-esteem wilts under her ceaseless criticism.[10]

The imagery used to describe Mrs. Tulliver is also suggestive of her connection with Maggie's oral frustration:

Mrs. Tulliver was what is called a good-tempered person— never cried, when she was a baby, on any slighter ground than hunger and pins; and from the cradle upwards had been healthy, fair, plump, and dull-witted; in short, the flower of her family for beauty and amiability. But milk and mildness are not the best things for keeping, and when they turn only a little sour, they may disagree with young stomachs seriously. (I, ii)

If such sourness frustrated the infant Maggie's early union with her mother, as the narrator obliquely suggests, and later disapproval hindered her narcissistic need from developing into a healthy self-esteem which

---

rushes to meet the Floss. The water with which he merges is part of a great fecund whole: the ships are bringing "rounded sacks of oil-bearing seed" and the earth is rich and "made ready for the seed of broad-leaved green crops." This aspect of the narrator will be significant when we examine the handling of the elopement with Stephen and the flood-death ending.

[10] "The Inner Conflicts of Maggie Tulliver," p. 173.

could take its place, it is understandable that Maggie remains "hungry" for love, and that her loving retains the quality of narcissistic need.[11]

Maggie's sex is another source of her low self-esteem.[12] Even her father, who takes pride in her intelligence as a reflection of his own, considers it a pity that she is a girl. In his opinion "an over-'cute woman's no better nor a long-tailed sheep" (I, ii). This image, coming from Mr. Tulliver, simply illustrates his idea of a useless anomaly. But it may also suggest in the author an unconscious connection between intelligence and long tails, so that intelligence in a woman becomes a denial of castration. In any case, Maggie's displays of intelligence, in the face of the judgment that such accomplishments are only appropriate for boys, constitute attempts to *be* a boy.

Since Tom is a male, and because in addition he is given the mother's love denied to Maggie, he becomes a crucial object for her. She tries to identify with Tom, and wants him to reciprocate by identifying with her. In Maggie's mind, the ultimate sense of well-being in-

[11] See Otto Fenichel, *The Psychoanalytic Theory of Neurosis* (New York, 1945), p. 40. "Certain narcissistic feelings of well-being are characterized by the fact that they are felt as a reunion with an omnipotent force in the external world, brought about either by incorporating parts of this world or by the fantasy of being incorporated by it ('secondary narcissism') . . . The longing for the oceanic feeling of primary narcissism can be called the 'narcissistic need'."

[12] Paris, p. 173, focuses on the social expectations of Mrs. Tulliver (Dodson) and the small town of St. Ogg's: "Not only are Maggie's aesthetic and intellectual faculties starved in the oppressively narrow medium of St. Ogg's, they are regarded as inappropriate for a girl and hence contribute to Maggie's uncertainty about her worth. She is not only a girl, and hence an inferior being; she is an inferior girl. In talents, manners and appearance, she is the opposite of what the Dodsons value in a female . . . "

volves no image of a mother (except as a womb), even though her need originates in a desire for the oneness of infant and mother. Tom replaces the mother in her idea of lost oneness. He resembles Mrs. Tulliver and possesses her love, and thus can substitute for her; and in addition he is a male, so that oneness with him means participation in his maleness and the end of castration anxiety. Thus Maggie's memories of early union go back to that perfect day of fishing at the round pool, when her passive oblivion was combined with Tom's approval: "it was enough that Tom called her Magsie, and was pleased with her. . . . Maggie thought it would be a very nice heaven to sit by the pool in that way, and never be scolded." (I, v)

Maggie's need to blur the distinction between male and female is apparent in her fantasy of being the queen of a child's world, "where the people never got any larger than children of their own age" (I, vii). Through this fantasy, and the situation in which it arises, we can see that Maggie's wish to be a boy is strengthened by her despair of ever living up to the ideal of femininity. To be the queen of her fantasy she would have to be "just like Lucy," but she can hardly hope for such a transformation. Her unruly dark hair, always a focal point in her mother's battle to change Maggie into a proper girl, has just suffered a painful contrast to Lucy's neat blonde curls. She decides to cut it off. Her action expresses rejection of her sex and a wish to rid herself of anxiety about it. When Maggie is described as looking like a small Medusa with her snakes cropped, the image suggests again (like the long-tailed sheep) the unconscious attitude of her creator. Freud interprets the snakes (hair) of Medusa as a "multiplication of penis symbols": in their numbers the cropped snakes relieve anxiety over the absence of one penis by replacing it with many, and their ability to grow back is added reassurance.[13]

Maggie's need to identify with Tom, to merge with him, is nearly always met with total frustration. She insists that Tom participate in her hair cutting, and he complies. But her misery begins when he laughs at her, and she has to realize how separate and different they are: "Tom was so hard and unconcerned; if *he* had been crying on the floor, Maggie would have cried too"[14] (I, vii).

A later castration scene, occurring when Maggie is approaching puberty, seems to result in an attempt to accept her difference from Tom. At school, Tom's pride has been severely shaken by his difficulties with Latin, so that he is "more like a girl" than ever before in his life, and even longs for Maggie's company (II, i). When she is due to visit him, he plans a little drama to impress her and build himself up. He borrows his drillmaster's sword with the intention of brandishing it before Maggie, making her believe that he is going to be a soldier. But when the time comes to exhibit the sword, Tom cuts his foot. Maggie's screams bring Mr. Stelling, who finds both the children on the floor—Tom in a faint, and Maggie crying beside him.

[13] Sigmund Freud, "Medusa's Head," in *The Standard Edition of the Complete Psychological Works of Sigmung Freud,* ed. James Strachey, 24 vols. (London, 1953-56), XVIII, 273; subsequently referred to as *Standard Edition.*

[14] I have included this quotation because it shows that Maggie not only wants to identify with Tom, but needs him to identify with her in return. In the later castration scene, we find her still attempting to identify with him, crying on the floor beside him after he injures himself—as she says here that she would do.

The sword scene is the culmination of a section which explores changes in Tom's feelings about himself, about Maggie, and about his deformed schoolmate, Philip Wakem. It is a section which increases our sympathy with Tom, and one immediate effect of Tom's injury is to elicit sympathy from Philip. But Philip's kindness and Tom's appreciation fade quickly, and our attention reverts to Maggie, for whom the castration scene seems to mark a more lasting change. At this point Maggie turns toward Philip, and identifies not with what she would like to be, but with something that resembles her own need:

Maggie, moreover, had rather a tenderness for deformed things; she preferred the wry-necked lambs, because it seemed to her that the lambs which were quite strong and well made wouldn't mind so much about being petted; and she was especially fond of petting objects that would think it very delightful to be petted by her. She loved Tom very dearly, but she often wished that he *cared* more about her loving him (II, v).

Thus Maggie can identify with Philip and try to accept him as a substitute for Tom.

We are asked by the narrator to admire Maggie's compassion, the result of "her own keen sensitiveness and experience under family criticism" (II, vi). But we are also made to see that Maggie's affection stems from her own need for love and approval, a kind of object love still dominated by passive aims, with little capacity for active giving or consideration of the loved object.[15]

[15] See Fenichel, pp. 84-85. "The early object relationships are complicated by the fact that direct erotic aims are as yet not clearly distinguished from the narcissistic aim of participating again in omnipotence. Consideration of the object begins to develop during the anal period. The earliest consideration, however, is still dominated by narcissistic aims and is ambivalent. The object is to be influenced by

Before Maggie's relationship with Philip has a chance to develop, there is a long separation during which Maggie passes into puberty[16] and experiences drastic changes in her outer and inner life. Her hunger for love has come under the influence of her asceticism, so that she must rationalize seeing Philip as altruism, something which will do him good. But she looks forward to "the affectionate admiring looks that would meet her ... to the certainty that Philip would care to hear everything she said, which no one else cared for!" (V, iii). Her "full lustrous face" looks down at Philip "like that of a divinity well pleased to be worshipped."

But Philip's need for a love that is more than pity, a need which he hints at continually, goes unnoticed by Maggie until his distress outweighs his diffidence and he makes an urgent plea for her love. Maggie wants to ease Philip's pain, but she can't make the kind of commitment Philip wants her to make, and grows uneasy under the pressure of his need. Her responses are first evasive, ambiguous, and even coquettish—all uncharacteristic of Maggie. Finally she makes a statement which is far from the profession of love Philip wants to hear:

What happiness have I ever had so great as being with you?— since I was a little girl—the days Tom was good to me. And your mind is a sort of world to me: you can tell me all I want to know. I think I should never be tired of being with you. (V, v)

---

every means available to offer the necessary satisfaction. If this is achieved, the object fuses again with the ego. Some neurotic persons remain fixated to this phase, governed by passive aims, incapable of any active consideration of the loved object. Behavior of this kind is also called narcissistic, though it is entirely different from the objectless primary narcissism."

[16] The symbolic connection between the failure of Maggie's father, and the stresses of puberty will be discussed below, p. 27.

It is a statement which shows that Maggie still compares Philip to Tom, and we can see that no matter how much Maggie needs the love and approval that Philip has to offer, she cannot be satisfied by someone as needy and dependent as herself.[17]

She still longs for the passive bliss of merging with a greater being, and one through whom she can also participate in maleness. Philip's deformity, which has acquired the significance of castration (through the imagery used to describe him,[18] and by association with Tom's accident), allows Maggie to see their meetings as "innocent" (V, i). Their first encounter in the Red Deeps occurs just after she looks up at "the broken ends of branches" of the old fir-trees, and Philip argues that their friendship "might bring about a healing of the wounds that have been made in the past." But once Maggie's ascetic defenses have been circumvented, her hunger for love is reactivated, and the desire to merge with a strong male also reappears.

[17] Paris, p. 185, quotes Karen Horney, *Neurosis and Human Growth* (New York, 1950), p. 244, to support this interpretation. I have found evidence in the novel to support it as well. But my point of view is indebted to his statement: "The weakness and dependency which make Philip so appealing to Maggie are also responsible for the absence in Maggie's feeling of the intensity that characterizes her relations to Tom and Stephen."

[18] See Reva Stump's analysis of the imagery used to describe Philip in *Movement and Vision in George Eliot's Novels* (Seattle, 1959), p. 95. "The most immediate cause of Philip's birdlikeness—his amorphous shape, his easily ruffled feelings, his helpless fluttering, his isolated sparrow-like residence on the housetop—is his humpback. This deformity, which makes Philip unfit to assume the masculine role in St. Ogg's, determines that he shall be brought up as a girl. . . . Throughout the book there are several indications of Philip's feminine characteristics, all underlined by the bird image. It seems reasonable to assume that this feminine quality is one of the reasons that Maggie is able to confide in Philip as she does but unable to love him except in a sisterly way."

Philip is disqualified, then, partly by his femininity. The description of the parting following Maggie's ambiguous profession of love gives Philip's inability to take Tom's place a visual embodiment:

Maggie smiled, with glistening tears, and then stooped her tall head to kiss the pale face that was full of pleading, timid love— like a woman's (V, v).

Afterward, Maggie experiences "a moment of real happiness," believing that "if there were sacrifice in this love, it was all the richer and more satisfying." Her happiness is in the approval her superego grants to self-sacrifice, and such approval can give Maggie a temporary feeling of well-being. But she goes home feeling that her "tissue of vague dreams must now get narrower and narrower" (V, v). "Richer and more satisfying" according to Maggie's superego is "narrower and narrower" according to her deepest desires.

Thus when Tom intervenes between Maggie and Philip and forbids their meeting, Maggie's anger[19] is accompanied by relief. The narrator comments that if Maggie felt relief "surely it was only because the sense of a deliverance from concealment was welcome at any cost" (V, vi). But the tone of his comment leaves room for the other reasons for her relief that we have had no great difficulty in uncovering.

By the end of Book V, Maggie has lost her only sources of love and approval: her father and Philip. After the death of her father, she decides to lead an independent life away from home. We cannot fully understand her decision, or begin to discuss Book VI, "The Great Temptation," until we explore another regressive

[19] The scene between Tom and Philip, and Maggie's angry response, will be discussed in Part II.

wish of Maggie's which is part of the condensed wish-fulfilling ending, and which can also be traced throughout the novel.

II

I have said that Maggie's wish-fulfillment involves a victorious reunion with Tom, in which she regains a lost love and proves her superiority over a rival sibling who is consequently destroyed. Maggie's intense love of Tom conceals not only Oedipal and narcissistic needs, but also hatred. The narrator's continual underlining of Maggie's love for Tom, which seems at first to give a curiously open emphasis to the Oedipal theme, is understandable as an attempt to cover up the deeply ambivalent nature of Maggie's love.

There is no admission or direct indication in the entire flood-death scene of Maggie's desire for victory over Tom. Maggie is presented as heroically altruistic: she forgets about her own lonely anguish as soon as her cry, "Which is the way home?" reminds her that her mother and brother might be in need of help (VII, v). From that moment she is filled with energy and the hope that this great calamity will remove the quarrel between herself and Tom. A "strong resurgent love towards her brother . . . swept away all the later impressions of hard, cruel offence and misunderstanding, and left only the deep, underlying, unshakable memories of early union" (VII, v).

Thus the commentary leads us away from any motive of revenge in Maggie. But exactly at this point the narrative turns from Maggie's feelings about Tom to focus on "a large dark mass in the distance." This mass turns out to be St. Ogg's, but it is just the first of the masses that finally capsize and drown Tom and Maggie. Now "for the first time distinct ideas of danger began to press upon" Maggie. She sees "floating masses . . . that might dash against her boat as she passed, and cause her to perish too soon" (VII, v).

The masses that finally capsize the boat turn out to be "huge fragments, clinging together in fatal fellow-ship," fragments of wooden machinery, "hurrying, threatening masses." These destructive masses are heavily emphasized. The word "masses" is used repeat-edly and modified by increasingly strong adjectives: "dark," "floating," "hurrying," "threatening"—until fi-nally "the huge mass was hurrying on in hideous tri-umph" after the disappearance of Tom and Maggie in the water. It is not until we relate that "triumph" to Maggie's psyche that we can understand the anal fulfill-ment in the flood-death scene. The destructive masses have been defensively separated from Maggie, I pos-tulate, and by examining Maggie's thoughts or the nar-rator's comments we can pick up little indication of the kind of triumph the author is unconsciously realizing through the rescue and drowning. But we must not forget that when Tom, once rescued, suddenly under-stands what has happened to him, he is "pale with a certain awe and humiliation." This represents a com-plete reversal of all previous confrontations between Tom and Maggie in the novel, and must be related to Maggie's long succession of humiliating experiences and to her awe of Tom. Maggie has never before been able to reverse the situation and come out on top.

Although it may be difficult to accept the destructive masses as symbolic of the release of Maggie's rage, it is not difficult to see that in all of her memorable inter-

actions with Tom there is evidence of unconscious anger. Her passionate childhood love of Tom reveals ambivalence indirectly, as part of the pattern of unintentional offense, cruel punishment, and ultimate forgiveness which we have already discussed in terms of oral
need. On the manifest level these interactions are always presented with an emphasis on Maggie's desire to
please Tom, and on the cruelty of Tom's severe response. Nevertheless, the repetition of "unintentional"
offenses suggests that unconscious resentment moti-
vates Maggie to hurt Tom. Her conscious desire to
please him and be at one with him prevents the admission of rage against him, but cannot prevent her desire
for revenge from producing offensive accidents.

Thus we find Maggie as a child forgetting to feed
Tom's rabbits, knocking over his house of cards, and
spilling his wine (all of which Tom adds to a list of past
offenses). At a more adult stage Maggie offends Tom
by seeking work too ostentatiously, and then by spoil-
ing Tom's moments of triumph, first by her secret
liason with Philip, which is discovered just as Tom is
about to repay his father's debts, and finally by drifting
off with Stephen Guest just as Tom is in a position to
buy back the mill.

These unintentional offenses never fail to result in
Tom's anger (which Maggie dreads above all things)
and cruel punishment in the form of the withdrawal of
love. The offense itself is one outlet for Maggie's unconscious rage, and the highly emotional condemnation
of Tom's severity is another. Maggie achieves a subtle
victory each time she provokes Tom to cruelty because
she can feel morally superior. When Tom finds out that
his rabbits are dead, his angry "I don't love you" is

considered "very cruel" by Maggie. Her response reveals her victory: "I'd forgive you, if *you* forgot anything—I wouldn't mind what you did—I'd forgive you and love you" (I, v). At the same time Maggie's words disguise her victory by emphasizing her love. The release of rage through the offense and the condemnation of Tom's severity allows Maggie once again to love, or at least to subdue her pride so that she can beg for the love she needs.

The whole pattern is repeated in the incident of spilling Tom's wine, pushing Lucy into the mud, running away to the gypsies, and then returning home to have all forgiven. It is repeated again in Maggie's secret meetings with Philip, the confrontation with Tom, and their reconciliation after Mr. Tulliver's death. The final repetition begins with Maggie's ultimate offense of drifting off with Stephen Guest: when she returns to Tom for punishment, he refuses to have her under his roof, so that with the coming of the flood Maggie gets the satisfaction of moral superiority in rescuing her harsh, unforgiving brother, and the unconscious hatred that George Eliot originally invested (but now denies) in Maggie culminates in their destruction by the threatening masses borne on the flood.

There is only one point in the novel when George Eliot permits Maggie to be conscious of her repressed hatred. After her father's failure, when she is deprived of all her pleasures, Maggie fears that she will become a demon:

She rebelled against her lot, she fainted under its loneliness, and fits even of anger and hatred towards her father and mother, who were so unlike what she would have them to be—towards Tom, who checked her, and met her thought or feeling always by some thwarting difference—would flow out over her affections and conscience like a lava stream, and frighten her with a sense that it was not difficult for her to become a demon. (IV, iii)

This moment of consciousness is manifestly attributed to unusual circumstances quite external to Maggie's psyche—the fall of her father into bankruptcy and illness, and the consequent loss of comforts and support. Maggie's suffering, at this time, is centered in her relationship to "the two idols of her life"—her father and Tom. She gets "no answer to her little caresses" from either one. As she tells Philip later, this is the "trial" she has to bear: "I may not keep anything I used to love when I was little. The old books went; and Tom is different—and my father. It is like death. I must part with everything I cared for when I was a child." (V, i)

If we shift our focus from Maggie to her author, we can see that she has created a situation which projects the blame for Mr. Tulliver's "failure" and Maggie's "privation" onto money. Ostensibly the Tullivers have "dropped below their original level" financially, and who's to blame becomes a preoccupation of the manifest content. Mr. Tulliver blames Wakem, Satan, and the world. The Dodsons blame Mr. Tulliver, as does Tom. Maggie hates blame, we are told, though she is certainly quick to blame her mother and "the Aunts" for their lack of sympathy. In fact the only possiblity for blaming that seems to be omitted from this crisis is Maggie blaming her father. But if we undo the author's projection of blame onto money, Maggie's "privation" and Mr. Tulliver's "failure" come together. What we find is the crisis of puberty, which brings not only a biological intensification of sexual impulses, but also a revival of infantile impulses, including oral need, anal rage, and Oedipal frustration and disappointment.[20]

Up until this crisis Maggie's relationship to her father is her one source of satisfaction. She seems, from the beginning, to have made Tom a substitute toward whom all her erotic impulses (oral, anal, and Oedipal) are directed.[21] But she has always had the father's love to turn to when Tom failed her. When the intensified demands of puberty upset this delicate balance Maggie finds her affections and her conscience overwhelmed by "fits of anger and hatred." Her subsequent development of a severe superego, after the discovery of Thomas à Kempis, becomes necessary as a defense against such feelings. At the same time, the severe superego, by turning rage inward against the self, becomes a substitute outlet for rage.

As a child, Maggie expresses rage rather directly (except toward Tom). When her mother prevents her from going with her father to bring Tom home from school,

[20] See Fenichel, pp. 110-11. "The relative equilibrium of the latency period lasts until puberty. Then there is a biological intensification of sexual impulses. . . . The psychological task in puberty is the adaptation of the personality to new conditions which have been brought about by physical changes. However, this task of adaptation would be less difficult if the new conditions were really entirely new. Actually they are similar to the experiences of the period of infantile sexuality and of the Oedipus complex. Therefore, the conflicts of these times also reappear. . . . The return of infantile sexual impulses is partly due to the fact that genital primacy has not yet been completely established, and puberty brings with it an increase in *total* sexuality; in part, however, the return of infantile impulses is caused by the child's fear of the new forms of his drives, which makes him regress to the old and more familiar forms. The asceticism of puberty is a sign of fear of sexuality and is a defense against it."

[21] I do not attempt here to review all the evidence pointing to an intense incestuous attachment between Maggie and Tom. The reader is referred to Smith's essay (see n. 5 above).

Maggie retaliates directly. First she defies her mother's attempts to curl her hair by dipping her head in a basin of water. Thereafter she brutally punishes a fetish doll. When she is outraged by Tom's attentions to Lucy, she pushes Lucy into the mud. And when her mother and aunts plague her about her unruly hair, she expresses her rebellion by cutting it off. This last action, while it is intended as a "triumph" over her tormentors, prefigures the later development of turning her rage against herself.

As an adolescent, however, Maggie takes a distinctly different attitude toward her impulses, especially rage. From Thomas à Kempis she learns that self-renunciation will end such "evil perturbations" and bring peace. But while Maggie seeks peace the action of the novel becomes suddeny more violent. The once violent Maggie, now an ascetic adolescent who abhors violence, becomes suddenly more violent. The once violent suggestively dramatize both the dread and the unconscious desires behind her strict asceticism. Her reactions to these scenes show intense participation which testifies to the force of repressed rage within her. They are both scenes of cruel abuse, one verbal, one physical, in which Maggie identifies with both victim and aggressor.

The first violent scene is a confrontation between Tom and Philip. Maggie has been seeing Philip secretly, and has often thought of being suddenly interrupted by her father or Tom—not because that was a likely event, but because "it was the scene that most completely symbolized her inward dread" (V, v). Her dread does not stop her from seeing Philip, but suggests an unconscious desire for the interruption. When Tom becomes

suspicious, he goes with Maggie to meet Philip, and
Maggie experiences "suffering in anticipation of what
Philip was about to suffer," so that "her heart beat with
double violence when they got under the Scotch firs."
As they "entered the narrow bushy path by the mound,"
Maggie's imagination, "always rushing extravagantly
beyond any immediate impression, saw her tall strong
brother grasping the feeble Philip bodily, crushing him
and trampling on him" (V, v).

There is no physical violence between Tom and
Philip, but Maggie's imagining of the scene is essentially
a beating fantasy in which the deformed Philip, with
whom she identifies, is physically assaulted by Tom.
The sexual meaning of the fantasy is conveyed symbolically by the topography: the phallic Scotch firs and the
feminine "narrow bushy path by the mound." Afterward, Maggie continues to feel Philip's pain ("it was
almost like a sharp bodily pain to her"). Her masochistic
involvement suggests that, as in the masochistic beating fantasy analyzed by Freud, the wish to be loved by
an Oedipal substitute (in her case, Tom) has become
condensed with and disguised by the need for punishment, thus producing the wish to be beaten by him.[22]

[22] "A Child Is Being Beaten," *Standard Edition,* XVII, 189. "If the genital
organization, when it has scarcely been effected, is met by repression,
the result is not only that every physical representation of the incestuous love becomes unconscious, or remains so, but there is another
result as well: a regressive debasement of the genital organization
itself to a lower level. 'My father loves me' was meant in a genital
sense; owing to the regression it is turned into 'My father is beating
me (I am being beaten by my father).' This being beaten is now a
convergence of the sense of guilt and sexual love. *It is not only the
punishment for the forbidden genital relation, but also the regressive substitute
for that relation,* and from this latter source it derives the libidinal
excitation which is from this time forward attached to it." (Emphasis
in original.)

At the same time, Tom's verbal attack, with its focus on Philip's deformity and Tom's pride in his own straight, tall masculinity, revives Maggie's resentment of her sex, which she sees as deformity, and in an outburst "of unsatisfied anger" she beats the floor with her feet and clenches her fists. Her orientation seems to have changed from masochistic to sadistic, here, just as the beating fantasies in Freud's analysis take a final sadistic form, originating in jealousy and sibling rivalry.

The verbal assault of Tom on Philip is succeeded by a confrontation between their fathers which actualizes the physical violence earlier imagined by Maggie. When the sight of his enemy throws Mr. Tulliver "into a frenzy of triumphant vengeance," he rushes on Wakem and flogs him fiercely with his riding-whip (V, vii). Maggie interrupts the scene, screaming "Father, father!" She pulls on her father's arm until he lets Wakem go. Mr. Tulliver then collapses in Maggie's arms and later dies, killed by the "dangerous force" of his own rage, while Maggie relives the agony of the moment over and over again.

This last scene is preceded by comments forboding the violence to come: how Mr. Tulliver, in a "paroxysm of rage" after one of Wakem's visits, had beaten the boy who served in the mill, just as once before he had beaten his horse. The beatings "left a lasting terror in Maggie's mind," and "the thought had risen that some time or other he might beat her mother" (IV, iii). This last idea, combined with the emphasis on interruption in both violent scenes, suggests that Maggie is dealing with elaborations of a revived primal-scene trauma.[23] She is left with the impression of sexuality as physical

[23] See Fenichel, pp. 92, 543, ff.

violence, a dangerous mixture of rage that can kill and forbidden Oedipal wishes that must be punished.

By the end of Book V, Maggie has found no way to sublimate any of her libidinal needs, or to resolve the conflict between those needs and her severe superego demands. The reconciliation with Tom at their father's death-bed represents no resolution of Maggie's conflict with Tom, a conflict which reflects her inner turmoil. She has lost not only her two sources of love and approval, her father and Philip, but also her defensive asceticism, while her fear of her libidinal desires has been heightened by the violent scenes. Her retreat from home and family after the death of her father is an attempt to remove herself from all temptation and to satisfy her superego at the expense of her libidinal desires. But this is not a workable solution. Maggie's retreat only serves to shift the balance of power.

III

So far I have shown George Eliot creating a complex heroine through whom she expresses oral, anal, and Oedipal wishes which we can share without anxiety largely due to the controlling presence of an omniscient narrator. In Books I-V, as long as Mr. Tulliver is alive, fantasy and defense seem quite well balanced. The narrator guides us toward identifying with Maggie, whose intense "wants," continually conflicting with hard reality, touch the inevitably frustrated infantile desires shared by all readers. And the anxieties belonging to such desires are eased by the omnipotent parental narrator, who says "we should not pooh-pooh the griefs of our children" (I, vii). After Mr. Tulliver's "downfall," the easy balance of the first two books is replaced by extreme tension as the conflict between desire and the real world becomes an inner conflict between wants and shoulds, id and superego. The uneasy feeling that Maggie's impulses are stronger than her inner controls is still assuaged by the narrator's ability to see the pride and impetuosity in Maggie's ascetic self-renunciation. But when her fear of impulse produces a sadistic superego, the narrator also begins to show signs of imbalance. He turns from an intensely sympathetic description of *The Imitation of Christ* as "a lasting record of human needs and human consolations" (IV, iii) to a defensive and bitter attack on "good society" where, apparently, "human needs" are not to be found:

In writing the history of unfashionable families, one is apt to fall into a tone of emphasis which is very far from being the tone of good society, where principles and beliefs are not only of an extremely moderate kind, but are always presupposed, no subjects being eligible but such as can be touched with a light and graceful irony. But then, good society has its claret and its velvet-carpets, its dinner-engagements six weeks deep, its opera and its faery ball-rooms; rides off its ennui on thoroughbred horses, lounges at the club, has to keep clear of crinoline vortices, gets its science done by Faraday, and its religion by the superior clergy who are to be met in the best houses: how should it have time or need for belief and emphasis? (IV, iii)

At this point the narrator's sympathy for Maggie's "large claims" begins to turn into idealization, and his detached vision of the world outside Maggie changes to personal bitterness and distortion.

The world that Maggie enters in Book VI, with its elegance and ennui, is an embodiment of this resentment. But before we explore the significance of this change, and the subsequent breakdown of control by the narrator, we should look at the latent content of the last two books.

After two years in a "third-rate schoolroom, with all its jarring sounds and petty round of tasks," Maggie's "hungry nature" (VI, iii) has the upper hand. She is not immediately able to "taste" the pleasures suddenly made available when she visits her cousin Lucy, but she finds "the image of the intense and varied life she yearned for, and despaired of, becoming more and more importunate" (VI, ii). Soon she feels "strong excitement" which is attributed to "the half-remote presence of a world of love and beauty and delight, made up of vague, mingled images from all the poetry and romance she had ever read, or had ever woven in her dreamy reveries" (VI, iii). Her imagination has transformed the sexual wishes associated with physical violence and danger into vague longings for love and beauty.

The language of Book VI brings the oral imagery of earlier books into sharp focus: both love and beauty are presented in terms of food for Maggie's "hungry nature." She tastes beauty in the form of "a riotous feast of music" (VI, iii) which "seems to infuse strength" into her limbs. When she is "filled with music" the voice of conscience is drowned out: a "weight" that she is ordinarily aware of carrying seems to be lifted. Her pleasure in music resembles the dreamy deafness of childhood when the roaring of the mill enveloped her, shutting out the rest of the world.

Love, like music, as long as it is restricted to regressive oral terms, can slip past the proscriptions of Maggie's somewhat exhausted superego and produce that special state in which the voice of conscience is drowned out. She has come to Lucy's with "a keen

appetite for homage" (VI, vii) and finds "the tribute of a
very deep blush and a very deep bow" from Stephen
Guest extremely agreeable. When Stephen catches her
after her foot slips, she finds it "very charming to be
taken care of in that kind graceful manner by some one
taller and stronger than one's self" (VI, ll).[24] Thus we
are prepared for Maggie's response to Stephen at the
beginning of their unintended elopement:

Maggie felt that she was being led down the garden among
the roses, being helped with firm tender care into the boat,
having the cushion and cloak arranged for her feet, and her
parasol opened for her (which she had forgotten)—all by this
stronger presence that seemed to bear her along without any
act of her own will, like the added self which comes with the
sudden exalting influence of a strong tonic—and she felt
nothing else. Memory was excluded. (VI, xiii)

This passage brings together all the previous indications of Maggie's longing to be passively taken care of,
to escape from the demands of conscience by merging
with a stronger being. She takes in love as "a strong
tonic," the ultimate nourishment. The giver of that love
is regarded not as an independent personality, but as an
"added self"—thus Stephen Guest is not named here:
he is a "stronger presence," a tonic which Maggie ingests.

24 We are told that "Maggie had never felt just in the same way
before," but she had certainly felt something quite similar at the round
pool when Tom took care of all the fishing operations and she had only
to dream on passively. Maggie's response to being taken care of by
Stephen at this point is the first indication that she will come to see
him as someone who can replace Tom (as Philip cannot). When Maggie
is alone with Stephen for the first time, Stephen offers his arm as they
walk in the garden, and the commentary expands on Maggie's earlier
feeling: "There is something strangely winning to most women in that
offer of the firm arm: the help is not wanted physically at that moment,
but the sense of help—the presence of strength that is outside them,
and yet theirs—meets a continual want of the imagination" (VI, vi).

We have also been prepared for the state of alarm and the rejection of Stephen which follow upon Maggie's passive oblivion. Her oral indulgence is both a regressive defense against the anal, Oedipal, and genital desires which terrify her, and a very fragile disguise for them. At the ball Maggie is able to "expand unrestrainedly in the warmth of the present, without those chill eating thoughts of the past and the future" (VI, x).[25] As long as Stephen speaks in tones of "subdued tenderness" which "bring the breath of poetry with them," Maggie is happy, and the trees and flowers in the conservatory "look as if they belonged to an enchanted land."

The poetry is disrupted when Maggie is drawn into sharing a "long grave mutual gaze." She tries to retreat from the meaning of that gaze, its sexual mutuality, by turning away from Stephen to the roses (and to terms of taking in, rather than giving):

"O, may I get this rose?" said Maggie, making a great effort to say something, and dissipate the burning sense of irretrievable confession. "I think I am quite wicked with roses—I like to gather them and smell them till they have no scent left." (VI, x)

But Stephen, instead of reverting to "subdued tenderness," carries the confession one step further. He has focused not on Maggie's words, but on her arm to which his response is not gallant, but overtly sexual: "A mad impulse seized on Stephen; he darted toward the arm, and showered kisses on it, clasping the wrist."[26]

[25] The revenge of Maggie's superego is also conceived in oral terms: "*eating* thoughts of the past and future" attack her after each indulgence (VI, x; my emphasis).

[26] Maggie's arm has already been given special attention by Mrs. Pullet as being "beyond everything" and much too large and round to fit into her aunt's sleeves, and by Mrs. Tulliver as being too brown to be "thought well on among respectable folks" (VI, iii).

Stephen's action destroys the enchantment Maggie is determined to preserve, and she responds "like a wounded war-goddess, quivering with rage and humiliation." Their "momentary happiness had been smitten with a blight—a leprosy: Stephen thought more lightly of *her* than he did of Lucy."

This encounter brings together the oral, anal, and Oedipal impulses explored in Parts I and II above. Maggie's rage reminds us not only of the pre-ascetic impulsive child who pounded nails into her doll and pushed Lucy into the mud, but also of the ascetic adolescent Maggie in Book V, who participated vicariously in the violent scenes between Tom and Philip, Mr. Tulliver and Wakem. The emphasis on Lucy here, with its implied admission of competition, again connects Maggie's rage and the oral passivity preceding it with Oedipal wishes. On the manifest level Maggie's sin ("the sin of allowing a moment's happiness that was treachery to Lucy, to Philip—to her own better soul") is self-indulgence at the expense of others. On the latent level her sin is Oedipal. The triangle between Stephen, Lucy, and Maggie is a recasting of the Oedipal triangle.

Lucy, as the injured third party essential to the Oedipal fantasy, is presented as playing the mother's role (and one which would please a Dodson mother): entering Maggie's bedroom in "ample white dressing-gown" she says, "Why, Maggie, you naughty child, haven't you begun to undress?" (VI, iii). And Maggie sees Lucy as "a fairy godmother" who has changed her "from a drudge into a princess" and who supplies all her needs: "I do nothing but indulge myself all day long, and she always finds out what I want before I know it myself" (VI, vii).

Thus Lucy represents, at one level, the mother who is

Maggie's Oedipal rival: Lucy not only plays a motherly role, she is preferred by Tom, who is the object of Maggie's Oedipal wishes. But Maggie's rivalry with Lucy is not only Oedipal. It goes back to Mrs. Tulliver's rejection of Maggie on the basis of her deviation from the ideal embodied in Lucy, which makes Lucy, like Tom, an envied rival for the mother's love Maggie desperately needs.[27] The negative feelings toward Lucy which would be only natural for Maggie under these circumstances are as deeply repressed as similar feelings toward Tom.

In the early books of the novel, Maggie's jealousy is, nevertheless, obliquely revealed when she pushes Lucy into the mud, and when she imagines living in an arrested child-world with herself as queen—but in Lucy's form. In Book VI, when the ugly duckling has emerged as a beautiful swan and the possibility of a vindictive triumph over her rival brings Maggie's buried jealousy dangerously close to the surface, these oblique revelations are replaced by denial. The narrator draws attention away from Maggie's jealousy by exploring the triangular situation through Lucy's feelings, rather than Maggie's

Is it an inexplicable thing that a girl should enjoy her lover's society the more for the presence of a thrid person, and be without the slightest spasm of jealousy that the third person had the conversation habitually directed to her? (VI, vi)

Maggie, instead of becoming aware of her buried jealousy, develops a dread of hurting Lucy, just as she has always dreaded Tom's anger—the dread growing

[27] Lucy is as clearly representative of the author's older sister, Chrissey, as Maggie and Tom are representative of Marian and Isaac Evans. Chrissey, like Lucy, was the pretty and docile favorite of her mother.

stronger as the unconscious impulse to bring about the hurt or the anger grows stronger.

At the beginning of her holiday at Lucy's, Maggie is so "absorbed" in experiencing her attraction to Lucy's lover that she has no energy left for thinking about it. As long as Lucy is present, Maggie and Stephen enjoy their discovery of one another freely. But after their first encounter alone, Maggie is left feeling the need of "a sanctuary where she could find refuge from an alluring influence which the best part of herself must resist, which must bring horrible tumult within, wretchedness without" (VI, vii). She hopes that Philip, who has just reentered her life, will be that sanctuary. He has become "a sort of outward conscience" to her, because he appeals "more strongly to her pity and womanly devotedness than to her vanity or other egoistic excitability of her nature."

But seeing Philip immediately revives the memory of a past conversation concerning her rivalry with Lucy, in which Maggie had declared her wish to "avenge" the "dark unhappy" women who always lost out to the blonde-haired heroines in novels. Philip's response had even then made her uneasy:

"Well, perhaps you will avenge the dark women in your own person, and carry away all the love from your cousin Lucy. She is sure to have some handsome young man of St. Ogg's at her feet now: and you have only to shine upon him—your fair little cousin will be quite quenched in your beams." (V, iv)

Maggie was hurt and defensive, because Philip's words touched unconscious jealousy:

"As if I, with my old gowns and want of all accomplishments, could be a rival of dear little Lucy, who knows and does all sorts of charming things, and is ten times prettier than I am—

even if I were odious and base enough to wish to be her rival."
(V, iv)

Maggie's sudden recollection of this conversation gives
"new definiteness to her present position" (VI, vii). Her
subsequent behavior fits Fenichel's description of the
"corruptibility of the superego," in which there is an
oscillation between concessions to the id and atonement:

If the ego makes a concession to an instinctual urge, it must
comply with demands for atonement; when it has atoned, it
may use the act of atonement to engage in other transgressions; the result is an alternation of "instinctual" and "puni-
tive" acts.[28]

Thus Maggie's rejection of Stephen after the arm-
kissing scene gives her a feeling of deliverance from
treachery against Lucy, and she retreats to her Aunt
Moss's, determined to follow duty rather than desire.
When Stephen unexpectedly appears there, she tries to
resist and does not succeed completely. Their argument
prefigures the arguments which lead to Maggie's final
rejction of Stephen, but for the time being Stephen is
able to confuse Maggie's rigid superego command not
to hurt others and not to be selfish by accusing her of
caring only for her own dignity and not for his suffering (VI, xi).

Maggie knows that her conscience will punish her
unmercifully if she follows her desires and Stephen's
urging that they should break their previous ties and
"determine to marry each other." She knows that her
inner turmoil cannot be ended by a victory of the
forbidden desires; but such knowledge does not give
her superego the victory either. It is corruptible. She
needs its approval, but her self-esteem is too weak to be

[28] Fenichel, pp. 291-92.

sustained for long by that approval alone. In the scene with Stephen at her Aunt Moss's, she tries to satisfy her conscience with earnest arguments on the side of duty, but at the same time her "hungry nature" makes her forgive him, take his arm once again, and indulge in one last kiss.

Maggie's corruptible superego repeatedly allows her to indulge her longing for love, as long as it is restricted to a passive oral mode. She cannot consciously decide to go away with Stephen, but she can passively submit until it is too late to avoid hurting others. Once she is on the river with Stephen, they do not speak: "for what could words have been but an inlet to thought? and thought did not belong to that enchanted haze in which they were enveloped—it belonged to the past and the future that lay outside the haze" (VI, xiii). Her first resistance results from a sudden change: Stephen stops rowing and Maggie looks around to see countryside that is strange to her. Immediately she is possessed by "a terrible alarm." In her passivity, as in earlier "fits of absence," she has come close to the desired oceanic feeling of the infant who feels himself at one with the mother. But when Stephen becomes passive, "watching the pace at which the boat glided without his help," Maggie becomes a "frightened child" surrounded by strangeness.

Stephen then becomes active again. He weakens her resistance, as he had done earlier, by indirectly accusing her of caring only for herself; and Maggie's corruptible superego is rendered powerless:

Maggie was paralysed: it was easier to resist Stephen's pleading, than this picture he had called up of himself suffering while she was vindicated—easier even to turn away from his look of tenderness than from this look of angry misery, that

seemed to place her in selfish isolation from him. He had called
up a state of feeling in which the reasons which had acted on
her conscience seemed to be transmuted into mere self-regard.
The indignant fire in her eyes was quenched . . . .(VI, xiii)

Maggie's paralysis is the outcome of an irresolvable
conflict between id and superego; her conscious ego,
unable to mediate between the claims of the two warring
parties in her nature, has become completely ineffective.[29] She can only temporarily escape from her inner
battle by yielding to Stephen:

Maggie was hardly conscious of having said or done anything
decisive. All yielding is attended with a less vivid consciousness than resistance; it is the partial sleep of thought; it is the
submergence of our personality by another. Every influence
tended to lull her into acquiescence: that dreamy gliding in the
boat, which had lasted for four hours, and had brought some
weariness and exhaustion—the recoil of her fatigued sensa-
tions from the impracticable difficulty of getting out of the
boat at this unkown distance from home, and walking for long
miles—all helped to bring her into more complete subjection
to that strong mysterious charm which made a last parting
from Stephen seem the death of all joy, and made the thought
of wounding him like the first touch of the torturing iron
before which resolution shrank.

Once they have boarded the boat going to Mudport,
Maggie's oral needs are satisfied: she walks "leaning on
Stephen—being upheld by his strength"; she is fed,
reclining on cushions and knowing that nothing could be
decided that day; and she receives Stephen's words of
love "like nectar held close to thirsty lips." Stephen's

[29] See ibid., p. 292. "The vacillation between deed and punishment is
frequently expressed in obsessive doubts, which really mean: 'Shall I
follow the demands of the id, or those of the superego?' Severe compulsion neuroses may terminate in states in which the conscious ego,
having become a football for the contradictory impulses of the id and
the superego, is eliminated completely as an effective agent."

words make her hope that there might be "a life for mortals here below which was not hard and chill—in which affection would no longer be self-sacrifice." And for the time being her vision of such a life "excluded all realities . . . all except the hand that pressed hers, and the voice that spoke to her, and the eyes that looked at her with grave, unspeakable love."

In this description of Maggie giving in to love, we can see not mutual giving, but passive receptive gratification. Stephen is still not a personality, but a "hand," "eyes," and "voice" which supply her needs. Nevertheless, during that night on the river something happens which gives Maggie the strength to leave Stephen. Her yielding turns to decisive resistance when a dream revives repressed wishes and points toward a course of action in which both id and superego can find satisfaction.

She dreams:

She was in a boat on the wide water with Stephen, and in the gathering darkness something like a star appeared, that grew and grew till they saw it was the Virgin seated in St. Ogg's boat, and it came nearer and nearer, till they saw the Virgin was Lucy and the boatman was Philip—no, not Philip, but her brother, who rowed past without looking at her; and she rose to stretch out her arms and call to him, and their own boat turned over with the movement, and they began to sink, till with one spasm of dread she seemed to awake, and find she was a child again in the parlour at evening twilight, and Tom was not really angry. (VI, xiv)

The first thing to notice is that in the dream Maggie moves away from Stephen and toward Tom. And it is in this movement that the condensation of superego demands for atonement with regressive sexual wishes is most apparent: the unconscious mind finds a way to make rejection of Stephen an act which will satisfy her superego, and at the same time satisfy her repressed Oedipal desire for Tom and her oral need to merge with a stronger male. The regressiveness of this solution is underlined by the movement backward in the dream from Stephen to Philip to Tom, and also by the conclusion, which finds Maggie and Tom as children in their childhood home.

Lucy is in an enviable position in the dream: she is the star, the Virgin, and the person for whom Tom ignores Maggie. Her position in the boat with Tom again underlines Maggie's unconscious jealousy, reemphasizes Lucy's role as Maggie's Oedipal rival, and calls up the casual suggestions that have been made earlier of Tom's frustrated love for Lucy.[30] But the dread of hurting Lucy, which has been Maggie's focus throughout the river journey, is not part of the dream. It has been replaced by Maggie's earlier dread of Tom's anger—which the dream wishes away: "Tom was not really angry."

It would be wrong, however, to conclude that Maggie's dream leads to a simple choice of her Oedipal love over non-Oedipal love. Maggie, for one thing, has never moved completely away from Oedipal love: her triangular situation with Lucy and Stephen has Oedipal overtones. But she has nevertheless encountered sexuality in terms that are new for her. In addition, she has found a love object who can satisfy her hunger for love (as Tom cannot) and her need for someone stronger and male with whom to merge (as Philip cannot). These

[30] See Maggie's interpretation of Bob Jakin's hints about Tom's loneliness: "It was a totally new idea to her mind, that Tom could have his love troubles. Poor fellow—and in love with Lucy too!" (VI, iv.)

enticements, offered by Stephen, might well prevail over an Oedipal attachment which, as we have seen, leaves her hungry for love—if it were not for the disapproval of her superego and the fear of sexuality. Her superego forbids most strenuously the satisfaction of vindictive wishes: she must not hurt others (and especially not the one who stands in the place of her original Oedipal rival—Lucy). The emphasis on *not* hurting others is not only a defense against repressed analsadistic wishes; it is also a displacement of the dread of being hurt herself through sexual assault. She wants "easy floating in a stream of joy" but fears the intense feeling she had when Stephen rode up to her on his "tall bay horse": "a beating at head and heart—horrible as the sudden leaping to life of a savage enemy who had feigned death" (VI, xi).

But once Maggie's dream has shown her the regressive path by which both id and superego can be partly satisfied, the enticements (and dangers) of her relationship with Stephen can be resisted. The condensation of regressive wishes with atonement has been observed by Fenichel as a possible outcome of the pattern of atonement and indulgence that he describes:

In defending itself against the demands of the sadistic superego, the ego may use a countersadistic rebellion as well as submission (ingratiation), or both attitudes simultaneously or successively. Sometimes the ego seems willing to take upon itself punishments, acts of expiation, and even torture to an astonishing degree. This "moral masochism" appears to be a complement to the "sadism of the superego," and this submission may be performed in the hope of using it as a license for later instinctual freedom. The ego's "need for punishment" is, in general, subordinated to a "need for forgiveness," punishment being accepted as a necessary means for getting rid of the pressure of the superego. Such a need for punishment on the part of a compulsive ego, however, may become condensed with masochistic sexual wishes. Then, in the words of Freud, morality, which arose from the Oedipus complex, has regressed and has become Oedipus complex once again.[31]

When Maggie wakes from her dream, she is still in the grip of the past and makes up her mind "to suffer" (VI, xiv). Her arguments to Stephen encourage us to think that she has finally been saved by her conscience: she could "never deliberately consent" to a choice of "conscious cruelty and hardness." Nevertheless, Stephen now has much more to combat than Maggie's corruptible superego. This time when he accuses her of thinking nothing of his pain and too much of her own, the device that has twice before confused her conscience and left her weakly passive toward him fails. Maggie maintains her position. But when she leaves Stephen she is not in a state that indicates a conscious decision, made after weighing alternatives. She is in a state very much like that of yielding to Stephen, only this time she is yielding to the combined forces of her need for punishment and her regressive id impulses, which are represented as the "tightening clutch" of the past:

Maggie was not conscious of a decision as she turned away from the gloomy averted face, and walked out of the room: it was like an automatic action that fulfills a forgotten intention. What came after? A sense of stairs descended as if in a dream— of flagstones—of a chaise and horses standing . . . and the darting thought that that coach would take her away, perhaps towards home. (VI, xiv)

Maggie still fears Tom's disapproval, but "she almost desired to endure the severity of Tom's reproof, to submit in patient silence to that harsh disapproving

[31] Pp. 292-93.

judgment against which she had so often rebelled . . ."
(VII, i). The resolution worked out in Maggie's dream
does not forsee Tom's actual reaction to her return, his
inability to forgive. His final insult, turning Maggie
away in her time of greatest need, calls forth the devastating flood, which adds the release of rage to the other
regressive fulfillments promised by Maggie's dream.

Maggie's indulgence of instinctual urges in drifting
away with Stephen demands a period of atonement, of
seeking punishment and making reparation. Her atonement is condensed with instinctual gratification, so that
her movement away from sexuality is at the same time
a movement toward unconscious masochistic sexual
wishes. Maggie's rescue of Tom from the flood enforces
his forgiveness, to complete the pattern of offense,
punishment, and reunion. The reunion is made lasting
by a death which satisfies Maggie's need for revenge
while it fulfills in its most ultimate sense her longing
for the oceanic feeling of submerging self in a greater
being.

So far I have been expanding the psychoanalytic interpretation of *The Mill on the Floss* in order to account
for the developments of the last two books, especially
Maggie's attraction to Stephen Guest, her return to
Tom, and the flood-death ending. When the latent content of the ending is exposed and seen as congruent
with the rest of the novel, the fact still remains that the
ending is anxiety-producing. In her letters George Eliot
defended the catastrophe, but she herself admitted "a
want of proportionate fullness in the treatment" of it.[32]
As I see it, this "want of proportionate fullness" is

---

[32] *The George Eliot Letters*, ed. Gordon S. Haight, (7 vols.; New Haven, 1954-55), III, 317; hereafter cited as *Letters*.

partly a failure of the form to provide the sense of control necessary to prevent the fantasy content from producing anxiety in the reader.

This is not to say that the fantasy content of *The Mill on the Floss* is ever blatantly exposed, or that there are no defenses against the forbidden impulses which constitute the latent content. I have already tried to show how the fantasy material is softened and disguised from beginning to end. But the inadmissable wishes at the end of the novel are so condensed that one lapse in defensive technique which occurs in the middle of Book VI is enough to cause uneasiness.

Throughout the novel, until the middle of Book VI, the narrator has been watching and explaining and criticizing everything and everyone, including Maggie. The reader, by identifying with the narrator, can control the extent of his identification with Maggie and thus distance himself from her conflict. But when Maggie begins floating downstream with Stephen, she is suddenly exempted from criticism. Maggie is still being described—the narrator still tells us what she says, does, and thinks. But Maggie's longings and her own moral reflections are no longer expanded or undercut by the objective and more experienced narrator.

In the fifty-six pages at the beginning of Book VI there are approximately seventy-five lines of objective critical analysis of Maggie (who is completely absent from fourteen of these pages). The comments here are penetrating, exhaustive, and omniscient:

Poor Maggie! She was so unused to society that she could take nothing as a matter of course, and had never in her life spoken from the lips merely, so that she must necessarily appear absurd to more experienced ladies, from the excessive feeling she was apt to throw into very trivial incidents. But she was even conscious herself of a little absurdity in this instance. It was true she had a theoretic objection to compliments, and had once said impatiently to Philip, that she didn't see why women were to be told with a simper that they were beautiful, any more than old men were to be told that they were venerable: still, to be so irritated by a common practice in the case of a stranger like Mr. Stephen Guest, and to care about his having spoken slightingly of her before he had seen her, was certainly unreasonable, and as soon as she was silent she began to be ashamed of herself. It did not occur to her that her irritation was due to the pleasanter emotion which preceded it, just as when we are satisfied with a sense of glowing warmth, an innocent drop of cold water may fall upon us as a sudden smart. (VI, ii)

By contrast, in the last fifty-six pages of the novel there are only twelve (as opposed to seventy-five) lines, four well-scattered sentences in all, which even come close to being objective critical comments of the previous kind. They are sentences such as this: "Maggie was half stunned—too heavily pressed upon by her anguish even to discern any difference between her actual guilt and her brother's accusations, still less to vindicate herself" (VII, i). This description hardly goes beyond what Maggie could have said about herself at that moment.

The abandonment of exhaustive and omniscient comment on Maggie—especially at this crucial point—gives the reader an insecure sense that the narrator's point of view has merged with Maggie's, and that the reassuring sense of control formerly provided by the narrator has vanished. The change occurs at the beginning of the thirteenth chapter of Book VI, "Borne Along by the Tide," when Maggie and Stephen drift off together. Maggie's passivity and submergence in the "stronger presence that seemed to bear her along without any act of her own will," and the "dreamy gliding in the boat," set a tone almost identical to the narrator's introduction to the novel in which he has dozed off before beginning to tell the story of the Tullivers. In his reverie, the narrator is "in love with moistness" and envies "the white ducks that are dipping their heads far into the water." He merges with the water, shares in the "impetuous embrace" with which the "loving tide" rushes to meet the Floss, and becomes part of a great fecund whole: the ships, bringing "rounded sacks of oil-bearing seed," and the earth, rich and "made ready for the seed of broad-leaved green crops" (I, i). Thus Maggie's longing to submerge herself seems to be shared by the narrator, and from the point in the novel when Maggie indulges this longing, the narrator loses objectivity.

At the same time the reader's feeling of insecurity is heightened by two other circumstances: first is the coincidental fact that Philip, another commentator on Maggie, disappears from the action in the middle of Book VI. Perhaps Dr. Kenn is intended to fill in the lack; but instead of supplying moral judgments, he argues against making them, on the grounds that "moral judgments must remain false and hollow, unless they are checked and enlightened by a perpetual reference to the special circumstances that mark the individual lot" (VII, iii).

Second, and far more significant, is the fact that the flood-death episode is an intense condensation of the various unconscious wishes embodied in the novel. As such, it would seem to demand an increase rather than a decrease in control. But instead of the objective narrator, we get several forms of disguise which work against each other. The first is an attempt to avoid

facing the implications of Maggie's renunciation by
blaming "society" (cf. pp. 29-30 above). As U. C.
Knoepflmacher points out, George Eliot is unable to
treat Maggie's "evasions of reality" as objectively as the
similar evasions of Mr. Tulliver:

Instead, significantly enough, the narrator now appropriates
the miller's hostility against the world at large. If Mr. Tulliver
foolishly blames "old Harry" for his own inability to find
fulfillment, our intelligent narrator is forced to blame a
different fiction—"the world's wife."[33]

The crude moral judgments made by "the world's wife"
seem to be supplied as a context in which Maggie's "act
of penitence" will inevitably take on heroic proportions
and thus escape undue scrutiny. We are not meant to be
aware of Maggie's renunciation of Stephen Guest as an
act of atonement which is condensed with masochistic
sexual wishes (see p. 42 above).

The emphasis on society as Maggie's opponent weakens the impact of the flood-death ending. The fulfillment of Maggie's regressive wishes is brought about
not by her own action, but by the action of the flooding
river. Thus her impulses are disguised by projection
onto an outside force. Such a projection, in itself, does
not prevent the flooding river and the nature imagery
leading up to the flood from successfully representing
forces of nature within Maggie, forbidden impulses
which can and do get out of control. But Maggie's inner
conflict has been obscured by the manifest emphasis on
society, where blame displaces analysis, so that the
well-foreshadowed flood seems to emerge out of nowhere, leaving the conscious preoccupations of the
novel unresolved.

[33] *George Eliot's Early Novels* (Berkeley and Los Angeles, 1968), p. 211.

Barbara Hardy argues that the novel "has a unity in imagery" which "has a strong mnemonic force, but . . . does not prepare us for the part played by the river in reaching the conclusion and solving the problem"[34] The implication of her argument is that the unifying nature imagery is a somewhat artificial superstructure, unrelated to what she sees as the heart of the story: "What we are prepared for is the struggle between the energetic human spirit and a limited and limiting society: such struggles are not settled by floods." What I have tried to establish above is a sense of the centrality of Maggie's *inner* conflict, which means that I see the heart of the story as the struggle *within* the "energetic human spirit." In terms of this struggle, the river imagery is not an artifical superstructure. It symbolizes the forces of nature in Maggie. But because of the gap between latent and manifest content created by blaming society, the dissatisfied reader is forced to choose betwen one level of meaning and the other.

There is a great deal of truth in Mrs. Hardy's claim that the "authenticity" of George Eliot's "analysis of moral choice" is undermined by the "shift into . . . blatant fantasy" at the end.[35] But if we look back through the novel we can see that the difficulty begins long before the flood-death ending. As Laurence Lerner observes, Maggie's renunciation of Stephen cannot be seen in terms of a simple contrast between principle and impulse: "Renunciation itself has been one of her strongest impulses."[36] Lerner considers the possibility

[34] "The Mill on the Floss," Barbara Hardy, ed., in *Critical Essays on George Eliot* (New York, 1970), pp. 46-47.

[35] Ibid., p. 50.

[36] *The Truth Tellers* (New York, 1967), p. 271.

that Maggie's impulsive renunciations "represent a sur-
render to a twisted but genuine selfishness," but his
terms cannot account for the dissimilarity between
Maggie's "pleasure in perverse self-denial and her drifting along with the warm tide of her feeling for
Stephen."[37] We need the concept of the sadistic superego, and an awareness of the ambivalence in Maggie
which makes it a corruptible superego, in order to see
how both drifting with Stephen and renouncing him can
be labeled "impulsive." When Maggie's dream shows her
the regressive path by which atonement can satisfy her
deeply repressed desires, the author's analysis of moral
choice faces an insurmountable obstacle. The unconscious would have to become totally conscious if she
were to pursue to the end the kind of analysis she began
with.

Thus it is not surprising that the omniscient narrator
is replaced by Dr. Kenn, who argues against making
moral judgments. Nor is it surprising that George Eliot
tries to muffle the sadistic and masochistic implications
of the devastating flood by deemphasizing death and
destruction and promoting the illusion of Maggie and
Tom as "living through again in one supreme moment
the days when they had clasped their little hands in
love, and roamed the daisied fields together." When this
evasion is added to those discussed above, we can see
why the ending of *The Mill on the Floss* has dissatisfied
many readers. But we cannot understand why so much
energy has gone into attacking, defending, and explaining that ending until we give due credit to its power.
The most remarkable thing about the novel is not that
it is imperfectly controlled, or that, as Leavis says,

[37] Ibid., p. 272.

George Eliot does not have "full self-knowledge," but
that she manages in the face of all her knowledge and
her principles to create the flood-death ending at all. It
is, as I said earlier, an explosive expression of conflicting
needs which, once objectified, changes the face of reality for the author and for any reader who attempts to
cope with it. It is not a breakthrough in the sense of
constituting a true self-confrontation. But it is a necessary first step. For Maggie, standing "at the entrance
of the chill dark cavern," the invitation to "life-
nourishing day" is rejected in favor of a death which
satisfies a sadistic superego and puts an end to inner
conflict. For Dorothea, standing "at the door of the
tomb," the possiblity of a life-affirming choice will de-
pend upon George Eliot's capacity to confront the somber implications of the self she expressed in Maggie.

Two

Silas Marner

Turning directly from the pages of *The Mill on the Floss* to *Silas Marner*, one experiences something like culture shock. Suddenly Maggie's conflicting needs, fears, and "shoulds" and the explosive rush of the symbolic flood-death ending are replaced by the apparent simplicity of Silas and the slow-moving symbolism of his isolated, insect-like existence.

This sudden shift away from the intensity and complexity of Maggie struck me at first as a defensive reaction—one for which there was sufficient cause in the novelist's circumstances. When she began writing *The Mill on the Floss*, even her best friends did not kow that Marian Evans Lewes was George Eliot. But before that novel was finished, the Liggins rumors had pressured her into revealing herself as the already famous author.[1] Thus the self-exposure of her highly autobiographical

[1] Gordon S. Haight, *George Eliot: A Biography* (New York, 1968), pp. 281-87; hereafter cited as Haight. It should be noted that the decision to drop the incognito was also influenced by the fact that the truth, "ferreted out by Chapman, was spreading generally in literary circles" (p. 287).

novel coincided with the public exposure of her irregular union with George Henry Lewes, and the sensitive author began to feel that she lived in a "house full of eyes."[2]

As long as I continued to view the shift to a reduced focal character as defensive only, thus treating *Silas Marner* as a realistic novel manqué, I could only regret losing the richness that was achieved in the portrayal of Maggie. But now I can see the shift as over-determined: it serves defensive purposes *and* expressive purposes. The simple, alienated weaver is not only reassuringly unlike the author, reduced to fit her defensive needs; he is also the vehicle for expressing a new understanding. And this symbolic function, which opens up if we respond to the non-realistic traces of folk tale as cues, is clearly of primary importance. As a symbol, the reduced character from whom "the movement, the mental activity, and the close fellowship"[3] of life have been stripped away, conveys a new awareness and a new valuation of the primitive human needs thus laid bare. And this new awareness constitutes a giant step toward reducing the opposition between id and superego which led to the death of Maggie.

Before coming to Raveloe, Silas Marner's life was "incorporated in a narrow religious sect" (chap. I, p. 7)—

    [2] Haight, p. 295. The Leweses took possession of Holly Lodge, their first home "after years spent in lodgings," on February 5, 1859, just after the publication of *Adam Bede* (pp. 272, 275). On July 23, not six months later, George Eliot wrote to her publisher: "When 'Maggie' is done, and I have a month or two of leisure, I should like to transfer our present house into which we were driven by haste and economy, to someone who likes houses full of eyes all round him" (*Letters*, III, 118).

    [3] George Eliot, *Silas Marner* (New York, 1962), chap. I, p. 7. Subsequent references are to this edition.

he was part of a community. When his trust in God and man was destroyed, he left the community. For the next fifteen years he lived outside the village of Rave-loe, having nothing to do with his neighbors beyond the selling of his cloth.

This is the bare outline of the first part of the Silas story, the action of the first two chapters of the novel. The imagery of these chapters suggests that Silas's alienation from society has meaning beyond the mani-fest emphasis on "the anguish of disappointed faith" (chap. I, p. 14) or its result in the shrunken life. In his aleination from Raveloe life, the simple weaver is com-pared to "the little child" who "knows nothing of paren-tal love, but only knows one face and one lap towards which it stretches its arms for refuge and nurture" (chap. II, p. 16). This metaphor not only points toward the later discovery of a little child; it also combines with the image of new land where "mother earth shows another lap" to suggest that Silas's first loss has to do with the child's loss of parents. Working with these images are the childlike qualities of Silas: he is repeated-ly described as "undersized," with an "expression of trusting simplicity" and a "defenseless, deer-like gaze" (chap. I, p. 9), and his lack of parents, his nearsighted-ness, his catatonic fits, and his overall passivity add to the impression of defenselessness. Thus "the anguish of disappointed faith" seems to have behind it the an-guish of the child without parents.

There are no actual parents involved in the flashback which accounts for Silas's outcast condition and esta-blishes sympathy for him. The eight-page sketch tells us that Silas is a victim, framed for robbery by his best friend, found guilty by God through the casting of lots,

and deserted by everyone including his fiance. But all
this has the appearance of a screen memory. There is a
peculiar emphasis on the triangular relationship between Silas, Sarah, and William:

> It had seemed to the unsuspecting Silas that the friendship
> had suffered no chill even from his formation of another
> attachment of a closer kind. For some months he had been
> engaged to a young servant woman, waiting only for a little
> increase to their mutual savings in order to their marriage;
> and it was a great delight to him that Sarah did not object to
> William's occasional presence in their Sunday interviews. It
> was at this point in their history that Silas's cataleptic fit
> occurred. (Chap. I, p. 9)

The juxtaposition of Silas's first fit with the engagement
and the triangle implies that the complete blocking of all
sensation represents the repression of feelings associated with a disguised or revived Oedipal conflict. This
implication is then borne out by rapidly succeeding
events—the death of a father-figure (during another of
Silas's fits), accusations of guilt from father-figures,
and the subsequent marriage of William and Sarah.

Thus the breach between the child and the parents
which underlies Silas's alienation seems to originate in
the Oedipal conflict. The child's competition with the
father or mother is doomed to failure and inevitably
gives rise to feelings of impotence and hostility, as well
as guilt. Silas's impotence is not disguised; in fact it
seems to be used to deny his guilt when he is accused of
robbery. His innocence depends upon two suppositions:
that the robbery occurred while Silas was in a catatonic
state (a state of perfect impotence), and that his pocket
knife, the incriminating symbol of phallic potency found
at the scene, was actually in the possession of William
Dane at the time of the robbery.

The guilt and hostility inherent in the Oedipal conflict *are* disguised, however, by displacement and projection. The emphasis on the robbery distracts attention from the fact that the senior deacon (an obvious father-figure) dies while Silas is keeping watch at his bedside. The hostility of wishing the rival parent dead is projected onto other father-figures, whose accusations are hostile acts against Silas. William Dane, Silas's closest friend (older and bigger than Silas, and "somewhat given to over severity"), becomes his first accuser, then the elders, and finally God himself.

Silas's actual father is never mentioned, and this omission gains significance from the displacement of attention away from the deacon's death. His mother is mentioned in regard to the knowledge of medicinal herbs she bequeathed to him at her death, knowledge which Silas has come to view as a temptation (along with his pleasure in gathering herbs) to underestimate the power of God (or the father). And the fact that this feeling akin to guilt can be admitted to consicousness, while feelings about the father are completely blocked out, implies that the strongest and most unacceptable feelings are associated with the father. This is indeed what the fantasy expresses by projecting the greatest part of the hostility onto father-figures. But hostility against the much desired but unfaithful mother is also projected. Thus, when Sarah marries William Dane, the Oedipal failure is complete, and Silas leaves Lantern Yard and regresses from the phallic stage.

Thus far the stress has fallen on the defensive function of the reduced character. At this stage of the fantasy the author's unconsicous and highly feared hostilities are projected onto characters outside the central, essentially passive character representing the author. Where we would expect to find guilt, jealousy, or hostility in Silas, we find instead the fits of blocked feeling. Silas is "unsuspecting"—he feels that his close friendship has "suffered no chill" from his engagement. When his friend suggests that his fits look like visitations of Satan, Silas feels no resentment (chap. I, p. 10). Thus Silas, like the hero of a fairy tale, is not allowed to be a whole or complex representation of the author; other characters, who represent the parents against whom he unconsciously feels hostile, are made to bear the hostile feelings. They wrong the central character, creating the breach between parent and child, and thus provide an excuse for the hostility with which they are unconsciously regarded.

But the ultimate aim of this defensive process (both here and in fairy tales) goes beyond such justification. For once the hostile parents have been punished, they can be forgiven and the breach between parent and child mended. It is this wished-for reconciliation between parent and child that is the most pervasive preoccupation in *Silas Marner*. It is evident in the fantasy fulfillments: one child-man (Silas) becomes both father and mother to a child; an abandoned child (Eppie) finds a motherly father; and yet another child-man (Godfrey) finds a mother substitute.

In the second stage of the Silas story the ground is prepared for the first of these reconciliations. The punishment of parents which, according to the fairy-tale pattern apparent above, precedes the reconciliation, is relegated to the Godfrey plot. Thus the healing of the breach for Silas seems to grow directly out of the regression which follows his break with the past. And this provides an important point of contrast with *The Mill on the Floss*.[4] When Silas leaves Lantern Yard, he cuts himself off from the past, and thus from parents and superego as well. He does what Maggie could not do, and what the author at the time could not conceive the value of. Thus Maggie's inner conflict could only be resolved in death.

Silas's death-in-life does not at first seem like a very promising alternative to Maggie's actual death. Raveloe provides him with a refuge because it is so totally unlike his native country and there is nothing to remind him of his painful past. Its strangeness is a buffer against thought and feeling, and his life is thus reduced to a few impulses: "He seemed to weave, like the spider, from pure impulse, without reflection," and hunger was also an "immediate prompting" which "helped, along with the weaving, to reduce his life to the unquestioning activity of a spinning insect" (chap. II, p. 17). But even while the narrative insists on the "narrowing and hardening" direction of this life which seems the opposite of growth, slight suggestions of hope appear. Silas's "rush of pity" for Sally Oates's suffering could not be "the beginning of his rescue from the insect-like existence into which his nature had shrunk," because he is not ready for the swarm of "mothers who wanted him to charm away the hooping cough, or bring back the milk" and "men who wanted stuff against the rheumatics or the knots in the hands" (chap. II, p. 20). But as Silas's

[4] For a lucid account of the differences and the kinship between aspects of the manifest content of the two novels, in terms which enrich this discussion of the latent relationship, see U. C. Knoepflmacher, *George Eliot's Early Novels* (Berkeley and Los Angeles, 1968), pp. 228-30.

life of "pure impulse" gradually develops the aspect of hoarding, his relationship to his guineas becomes a demonstration and a discovery that regression can be creative if it reestablishes vital contact with primitive needs.

When hoarding becomes an established habit, Silas's regression is a stabilized and completed form:

So, year after year, Silas Marner had lived in this solitude, his guineas rising in the iron pot, and his life narrowing and hardening itself more and more into a mere pulsation of desire and satisfaction that had no relation to any other being. His life had reduced itself to the functions of weaving and hoarding, without any contemplation of an end towards which the functions tended. (Chap. II, p. 22)

At first it is merely "pleasant to him" to feel the guineas in his palm "and look at their bright faces, which were all his own" (chap. II, p. 18). Then he develops a "habit of looking towards the money and grasping it with a sense of fulfilled effort." The spider weaves a web out of his bodily contents, and Silas is "like the spider." He exchanges the "brownish web"—produced by "his muscles moving with such even repetition that their pause seemed almost as much a constraint as the holding of his breath" (chap. II, p. 24)—for golden guineas which he cherishes as "all his own," representative of nothing outside himself.

The connection of the guineas to anality is evident not only in the spider metaphor (the brownish web and bodily contents), but also in the cluster of images related to Silas's hoarding activities: the stone pits filled with red water, the hole at his feet where he hides the gold, the brown pot that becomes a memorial, the iron pot and two leather bags (with their "dark leather mouths") which hold his gold, and later also the coal hold where he puts Eppie for punishment. Raveloe itself, situated in a "rich central plain," "nestled in a snug, well-wooded hollow" with "well-walled orchards" (chap. I, p. 7), is cloacal (womb-like and anal):

Nothing could be more unlike his native town, set within sight of the widespread hillsides, than this low, wooded region, where he felt hidden even from the heavens by the screening trees and hedgerows. (Chap. II, p. 16)

It is at once completely strange and a refuge, "another lap."

Behind this portrayal of Silas's anality, and despite the generally cool detachment which governs it, there is a mixture of conflicting attitudes: an insatiable interest in the hoarding which is evident only in the way the repeated details stand out against the strict economy of the work, a stress on the progressive dehumanization "into a *mere* pulsation of desire and satisfaction" which implies that the process is deplorable, and an almost reluctant admission that something positive is happening. If Silas had had a "less intense nature," we are told, he might have "sat weaving, weaving" (chap. II, p. 21), without becoming interested in the gold. As it is, the guineas become more and more important:

. . . the money not only grew, but it remained with him. He began to think it was conscious of him, as his loom was, and he would on no account have exchanged those coins, which had become his familiars, for other coins with unknown faces. He handled them, he counted them, till their form and colour were like the satisfaction of a thirst to him; but it was only in the night, when his work was done, that he drew them out to enjoy their companionship. (Chap. II, p. 21)

Their significance gradually changes until they are not merely anal products, but children "begotten by his labor" (chap. II, p. 24). But it is not until Silas has lost his gold that the narrative explicitly recognizes the fact that Silas's hoarding is an expression of "his power of loving" (chap. V, p. 50). Only when it has been brought to an end is the hoarding recognized as an activity which leads to his rescue by fostering his "power of loving."

Perhaps this explicit recognition has been withheld consciously, in order to bring the reader along very, very graudally. But I doubt it. That is why I have called the exploration of Silas's relationship "a demonstration and a discovery" (see p. 62 above). The idea that "the sap of affection was not all gone" from Silas, even at this stage, is certainly presented explicitly. But the author chooses an incident not obviously related to the hoarding to symbolize it—his preservation of the broken pot as a memorial of twelve years of companionship. His nightly "revelry" is juxtaposed to this incident, but there is a note of shock in it: "How the guineas shone as they came pouring out of the dark leather mouths!" (chap. II, p. 23). Then the tone softens again when Silas's view of them as children is described:

He loved the guineas best, but he would not change the silver—the crowns and half-crowns that were his own earnings, begotten by his labour; he loved them all. He spread them out in heaps and bathed his hands in them; then he counted them and set them up in regular piles, and felt their rounded outline between his thumb and fingers, and thought fondly of the guineas that were only half earned by the work in his loom, as if they had been unborn children . . . (Chap. II, p. 24).

With this new significance of the guineas as children, Silas's possessive feelings, even before Eppie replaces the gold, have essentially progressed from himself to an outside object, from feces to child. This progression, which is preceded by the regressive change of object from penis to feces, is a typical formula for the normal development of a female Oedipal complex. The regression from genital to anal eroticism is one means by which the female child can move from penis envy and the mother as the object of her phallic wishes, toward the desire for a child and the father as the object of receptive wishes. Thus through a male character a female author represents her own emotional development, which has an early masculine stage. Silas is designated as a man, but one who is not only impotent but also "partly as handy as a woman" (chap. XIV, p. 165); he does not represent at any time a completely masculine or a completely feminine character. When Eppie replaces his gold, he becomes both father and mother to her.

But before the coming of Eppie, another important change takes place which moves Silas another step toward life and growth. He is robbed of his gold.[5] When his initial disbelief at the sight of "the empty hole" gives way to the realization of his loss, Silas "put his trembling hands to his head, and gave a wild ringing scream, the cry of desolation" (chap. V, p. 52). He has lost his gold children, but he himself utters the primal scream of the

[5] This section, in which the narrative returns to the story of Godfrey and Dunstan Cass, has a slightly different tone from that dealing with Silas's hoarding. The first pages of Chap. V present Silas's thoughts and acitons with more ordinary variety of detail than we have seen: "Silas was thinking with double complacency of his supper: first, because it would be hot and savory; and secondly, because it would cost him nothing. For the little bit of pork was a present from that excellent housewife, Miss Priscilla Lammeter, to whom he had this day carried home a handsome piece of linen . . . " This change adds to the impression that the posture of holding Silas at arm's length belongs to the tension of mixed repulsion and fascination which relaxes when the gold disappears.

abandoned child. The robbery has left him "a second time desolate," and what an increase in intensity there is between his first protest—"there is no just God that governs the earth," uttered "in a voice shaken by agitation" (chap. I, p. 13)—and this "wild ringing scream"!

The robbery forces Silas to reach out to his neighbors for the first time since the miscarriage of his compassion for Sally Oates:

This strangely novel situation of opening his trouble to his neighbours, of sitting in the warmth of a hearth not his own, and feeling the presence of faces and voices which were his nearest promise of help, had doubtless its influence on Marner, in spite of his passionate preoccupation with his loss. Our consciousness rarely registers the beginning of a growth within us any more than without us: there have been many circulations of the sap before we detect the smallest sign of the bud. (Chap. VII, p. 69)

This commentary may discount the growth that was taking place in Silas even before the robbery. The emphasis generally falls on the gold as an obstacle: Silas's hoarding had "fenced him in" from the outside world, because the object of his "clinging" was "a dead disrupted thing." But the commentary does recognize that in spite of its deadness, the gold "satisfied the need for clinging" (chap. X, p. 94). And the effect of its loss depends on the love it has acquired. Thus, although Silas could not respond directly to the new kindliness of his neighbors, the "bewildering separation from a supremely loved object" led to "the habit of opening his door and looking out from time to time, as if he thought that his money might be somehow coming back to him" (chap. XII, p. 137). And that open door—with a little help from "the invisible wand of catalepsy" (chap. XII, p. 138)—makes it possible for the real child to enter his life.

When George Eliot describes that fit which arrests
Silas at his open door as "the invisible wand of catalepsy" she is deliberately drawing attention to her use
of fairly-tale elements in the novel.[6] This touch of mystery leads up to the greater mystery of Eppie's intrusion, and we are not meant to miss the symbolic import
of these events. They are not "miracles" in the sense
that they originate in supernatural forces. Each one, as
David R. Carroll points out, is a "natural event which
simply crystallizes a human process that has been going
on for some time."[7] The author has carefully given a
detailed natural account of how Eppie arrived at the
stone cottage, and an equally detailed account of the
changes in Silas prior to Eppie's appearance. In a sense
Silas's regression to a life of "pure impulse" is a process
of rediscovering the child in himself, the primitive self
from which a loving human being and even a religious
faith may grow if nurtured. Silas is ready for Eppie, but
the conjunction of her appearance with Silas's open
door and closed senses is still mysterious, and the mystery is underlined. It is necessary, not as a literary
device, but as an element of meaning. Eppie's coming
symbolizes the intrusion on the facts of life of the
mysterious process of life itself, the interruption of our

6 The fairy-tale devices have led some critics, notably Jerome Thale,
to object that the regeneration of Silas is a reflection of wishes rather
than a serious reflection of life. This objection disregards the importance of the changes in Silas leading up to the appearance of Eppie, and
disregards the capacity of the fairy tale, with all its wish-fulfilling
miracles and metamorphoses, to symbolize the mysterious and
wonderful aspects of human experience which are beyond the reach
of stick-to-the-fact realism. See Thale, "George Eliot's Fable for Her
Times," *College English* 19 (1958): 144.

7 "*Silas Marner*: Reversing the Oracles of Religion," in *Literary
Monographs*, ed. Eric Rothstein and Thomas K. Dunseath (Madison,
1967), I, 188.

daily struggles by awesome "beauty in the earth or sky" or the equally wonderful "wide-gazing calm" of a child (chap. XIII, p. 148). The comprehensible and the incomprehensible combine to bring Silas and Eppie together, and the result is not a mere reflection of life, but a conception of life as an interaction between the forces of nature in man and the forces of nature outside man, both of which have aspects as mysterious even to the educated mind as "the rain and the harvest" is to Dolly Winthrop.

At the level of fantasy, Eppie's coming to Silas is the fulfillment of the child's longing for parental love, expressed both directly in Eppie's discovery of Silas, and through reversal in his discovery of her. When Eppie comes on the scene, however, the relationship between the manifest content and the latent content changes. The underlying wish-fulfillment finds a new vehicle in Eppie's prosperity under the "perfect love" of her "almost inseparable companionship" with Silas (chap. XVI, p. 181). She is a more obvious version than Silas of the outcast child. And once again the child's hostilities are projected onto parents—a mother who leaves her exposed in the snow, and a father who won't own her. Her rescue by Silas, who makes his stone hut into "a soft nest for her, lined with downy patience," and who nurtures her like a mother, is an undisguised fantasy.

Silas's "unfolding" parallels Eppie's, but with an added dimension which is the focus of George Eliot's interest: Silas's awakening senses bring about awakening faith. The details of this slow process do not, however, point to another stage of fantasy fulfillment for Silas. Eppie reminds him of his little sister, and thus begins a reuniting of his past life with the present which is part of the reconciliation fantasy. But most of the imagery is used to portray the natural growth of Silas's new religious feeling.

The focus on religion is not a displacement meant to draw attention away from the fantasy, but an elaboration of the fantasy. This unique harmony between manifest and latent concerns is apparent in Carroll's description of Silas's "gradual recreation of a valid mythology":

Silas's love for Eppie, as it develops, slowly gains religious accretions which add up at the end of the novel to a complete trust in a new God. George Eliot shows how these accretions are not extraneous, supernatural additions, but rather mythical expressions of the human love which is firmly at the center of this new religion.[8]

Silas's groping for meaning is the expression of a need as basic to human nature as the child's need for parental love, a need which Suzanne Langer calls "the *need of symbolization.*"[9] Its working is epitomized in the process by which Silas's hearth, where he found Eppie, becomes symbolic and almost sacred to him: "Silas would not consent to have a grate and oven added to his conveniences: he loved the old brick hearth as he had loved his brown pot—and was it not there when he had found Eppie?" (chap. XVI, p. 176).

When George Eliot points out this "fetishism," her concern is to show, through the smallest act of symbolization, how true religious feeling grows out of human love. In the same way Eppie's decision to stay with Silas rather than go with Godfrey demonstrates the relationship between morality and love: her resolution was

[8] Ibid., p. 184.
[9] *Philosophy in a New Key* (New York, 1951), p. 45, (emphasis in original).

determined not by "thoughts, either of past or future," but "by the feelings which vibrated to every word Silas had uttered" (chap. XIX, p. 213). Through a progression of demonstrations like these, the fantasy of reunion between parent and child is manifestly elaborated as a view of life which replaces the fear of impulse and the control of "shoulds" with a new order based on "tenderly-nurtured unvitiated feeling" (chap. XVI, p. 182).

There are, of course, elements of the fantasy fulfillment which do not fit into this transformation of fantasy into meaning. Eppie's fondest wish—to live happily ever after with her father—is granted, and the parent-child reunion regains the Oedipal overtones of the early part of the Silas story. Silas is not Eppie's real father, and there are traces of a lively coquettish and competitive relationship with Aaron, who becomes Eppie's husband. Thus the Oedipal wish is somewhat disguised. But if we look at the end of the story the husband is conspicuously hard to find. It is almost as though Eppie and her father were being married. The description of the wedding procession mentions coolly that Eppie had one hand "on her husband's arm" while more warmly "with the other she clasped the hand of her father Silas" (Conclusion, p. 225). Eppie's last words leave her husband out completely, as though he were paired off with his mother instead of his new wife: "Oh, Father," said Eppie, "what a pretty home ours is! I think nobody could be happier than we are" (Conclusion, p. 227). Actually Eppie would have preferred not to marry or make any change. After all, as she argued to Aaron, her father had never been married. But since she will need help when Silas gets too old to work, Eppie takes the view that Aaron will be a son to Silas. Of course to some extent this reasoning reflects Eppie's sensitivity to Silas's dependence on her. But the Oedipal wish remains. The fantasy ends in a marriage, a peculiar sort of family marriage frequently met with in fairy tales.

The ending of the plot centering around Godfrey Cass does not have this fairy-tale quality. The Silas story is, at critical points, presented in absolute terms—extremes which set it apart from ordinary experience and at the same time give it symbolic power. At first Silas is absolutely devoid of jealousy and hostility, then he is absolutely cut off from his past, and later he is absolutely desolate (as during his fits he is absolutely helpless). Godfrey's story, on the other hand, is not characterized by absolutes. He has the same need for love as Silas, but it is so deeply enmeshed with the hostility and the fears resulting from its frustration that his development takes a very different turn. His life is not isolated and reduced, but socially bound, and thus his story demands, and lends itself to, a more realistic treatment than the Silas story.

Nevertheless, at the fantasy level there are striking similarities between the two plots. At one level Godfrey is another version of the parentless child. His father is alive, but does not provide either the love or the sense of order that he needs: "he had always had a sense that his father's indulgence had not been kindness, and had had a vague longing for some discipline that would have checked his own errant weakness and helped his better will" (chap. IX, p. 88). Godfrey's mother died when he was a child, and Nancy Lammeter represents to him the mother he longs for. In his thoughts she is always associated with the order and firmness of purpose he

misses in his father's house "without that presence of
the wife and mother which is the fountain of whole-
some love and fear" (chap. III, p. 26). In fact, Nancy
represents not only domestic order, but also inner
order—that "discipline" which could rescue Godfrey
from his own weakness:

> ... she would be his wife, and would make home lovely to him,
> as his father's home had never been; and it would be easy, when
> she was always near, to shake off those foolish habits that were
> no pleasures, but only a feverish way of annulling vacancy.
> (Chap. III, p. 37)

Thus what Godfrey fears is his own impulsive self. It
has led him into marriage with Molly—the "blight" on
his life. What he wants is a superego strong enough to
overpower the "low passion" he despises in himself. His
degrading marriage has made him "an outlawed soul"
like Maggie, who felt doomed to "sink and wander
vaguely, driven by uncertain impulse" if she let go of
the sacred ties of the past.[10]

Godfrey's daydream of being rescued by Nancy
equates his marriage with Molly to being "dragged back
into mud and slime" while he should have kept "fast
hold of the strong silken rope by which Nancy would
have drawn him safe to the green banks, where it was
easy to step firmly" (chap. III, p. 37). This rescue from
the water by means of a "strong silken rope" is clearly a
birth fantasy in which Godfrey sees Nancy as mother.
But the birth is a return to mother and "paradise" rather
than an entrance into the world.

The parent-child relationship is seen as a refuge from
the dangers of sexuality, and Godfrey's flight from
sexuality toward a mother figure is just as clearly a

[10] *The Mill on the Floss,* VI, xiv.

regression as Silas's anal hoarding. Both characters abandon genital sexuality and find refuge in parent-child relationships. Godfrey's fear of sexuality is less disguised than Silas's; his guilt has a physical embodiment in his secret marriage, and his hostility is apparent in "cruel wishes, that seemed to enter, and depart, and enter again, like demons" (chap. III, p. 38). Unlike Silas, he is aware that he is not simply a victim:

If the curses he muttered half aloud when he was alone had no other object than Dunstan's diabolical cunning, he might have shrunk less from the consequences of avowal. But he had something else to curse—his own vicious folly . . . (Chap. III, p. 36)

But the "jealous hate" and "cupidity" which are Dunstan Cass's only qualities, and his only motivation for tormenting Godfrey, seem nevertheless to be defensive projections. Dunstan's fate is the fate from which Godfrey is rescued in the birth fantasy: he is literally "dragged back into the mud and slime" at the stone pits and drowned. The horse and whip which he takes from Godfrey, like the knife which William Dane takes from Silas, are symbols of the feared sexuality from which Godfrey retreats. They represent the phallic self which Godfrey gives up in order to avoid another kind of castration—being "cut off from his inheritance" and from his mother-rescuer: losses which would leave him "as helpless as an uprooted tree" (chap. III, p. 32).

The basic similarity in fantasy content of the two plots constitutes a basis for pondering the significance of their differences. The fantasy elements of the Godfrey plot which are less disguised than their parallels in the Silas story are evidence of the defensive function of the double plot. The fragmentation is a disguise which helps

to prevent the fantasy content from emerging too bold-
ly, as it does in the end of *The Mill on the Floss*. Thus the
punishment of parents which is missing from the Silas
story is played out in the Godfrey plot. Godfrey Cass is
not only a parentless child at the fantasy level; he is also a
parent, and his failure—as a parent—to acknowledge his
child is one of the differences between Silas and Godfrey
that account for their dissimilar fates.[11]

But in regard to the new awareness that I have postu-
lated, and its relationship to *The Mill on the Floss*, there is
a more significant difference between the two plots.
Godfrey and Silas both find refuge in the parent-child
relationship, but Silas first undergoes fifteen years of
complete isolation. When he denounces God and man,
he cuts himself off from the past and from the structure of mind belonging to parents and authorities—the
superego. Thus, when he begins to grow again, the new
ties and new faith grow out of the primitive needs to
which he has been reduced. But Godfrey bypasses this
whole process. He manages to avoid being cut off completely, and he does this by clinging to Nancy Lammeter
and her absolute ideas. He adopts her strong superego,

---

[11] According to Carroll's interpretation of the manifest content,
most of which I find extremely convincing, Godfrey's regeneration is
less complete than Silas's because, unlike silas, he has wished harm upon a fellow human being, and "it is this which accounts for the different endings of the two stories: Silas's story ends in happiness and fulfillment, Godfrey's in understanding and partial disillusionment." (op.
cit., p. 181). But this interpretation seems to jar with the relative importance given to Molly and Eppie. Even at the manifest level, the fact
that Godfrey wishes Molly dead is not given half the stress that his
failure as a parent to love and acknowledge his child is given. It seems
to me, at least, that when the fantasy and the moral discourse are
viewed together, Godfrey's incomplete happiness is more closely
related to his failure as a parent than to his inability to repress as
completely as Silas his hostile wishes.

the "unalterable little code" that will restrain his feared impulses. As a result Godfrey, for the next fifteen years, is cut off—not from others (as Silas is), but from his own primitive self. Thus, when he finally acknowledges his past errors to Nancy and decides to lay claim to Eppie, his own child (symbolic of that self) is no longer accessible to him. The discovery of Dunstan's skeleton (with Godfrey's whip) represents to some extent a return of that self and of masculinity. For the first time he is strong enough to dare offending and losing Nancy by telling the truth—to dare losing his mother for the sake of his own being. But the process of reintegration of the self is not completed within the confines of the novel.

When the different fates of Godfrey and Silas are presented in these terms, we can see more clearly how *Silas Marner* reevaluates the opposing forces of id and superego which led to the death of Maggie. But I do not mean to suggest that George Eliot's new vision grew out of a conscious perusal of the implications of Maggie's irresolvable conflict. Her letters and journals provide ample evidence to the contrary. Her next novel, after *The Mill on the Floss*, was to be set in fifteenth-century Florence and centered on the life of Savonarola—apparently as far removed as possible from the sorrows of Maggie and the author's personal life. But while she labored over her research, despairing of ever knowing enough to begin writing, something unexpected happened. Her work was interrupted by a "sudden inspiration," she wrote to her publisher, "a story of old-fashioned village life, which has unfolded itself from the merest millet-seed of thought."[12]

12 *Letters*, III, 371. See also Lilian Haddakin, "*Silas Marner*," in *Critical Essays on George Eliot*, ed. Barbara Hardy (New York, 1970), p. 60.

A notation in George Eliot's journal suggests that the story not only unfolded itself, but emerged from her unconscious rather importunately, as if it represented a neglected self which demanded a hearing:

I am engaged now in writing a story, the idea of which came to me after our arrival in this house, and which has thrust itself between me and the other book I was meditating.[13]

Her childhood impression of "a linen-weaver with a bag on his back"[14] was no doubt revived by her own feeling of alienation, and her complex response to that strange image from the past is embodied in the novel. In writing *Silas Marner* George Eliot was not translating an idea into a picture, but using a picture to discover meaning.

The story of Silas's reduced life explores from many angles what the primitive side of man *is*—what our most primitive nature consists of. To the "brawny country-folk" of Raveloe Silas is one of those "pallid undersized men" who look "like the remnants of a disinherited race" (chap. I, p. 1). His uncanny effect on his neighbors is stressed, and the explanations offered rely heavily on the inexperience of the "rude mind" and on the rural isolation of Raveloe, where "echoes of the old demon-worship" still lingered, and imagination was "all overgrown by recollections that are a perpetual pasture to fear" (chap. I, pp. 3-4). The point seems to be that Silas is feared because the villagers of Raveloe are so primitive. But, on the other hand, it is Silas who looks like a primitive remnant. And Freud's comment that the "uncanny is in reality nothing new or alien but something which is familiar and old-established in the

---

13 *Letters*, III, 360.
14 Ibid., p. 382.

mind and which has become alienated from it only by the process of repression"[15] opens up another possibility. Perhaps Silas is feared by the villagers not because they are so primitive, but because *he* is so primitive, an unwelcome reminder of their own disinherited and disavowed primitive selves.

This "perhaps" leads to another. Perhaps the author herself had this response to the revived image of the linen weaver, a response which she symbolized in the cataleptic fits which made the villagers of Raveloe look upon Silas as "a dead man come to life again"—a striking image for the return of the repressed. If so, the legendary quality of *Silas Marner* preserves the sense of mystery which belongs to such a subject, while the intermingled thread of realism makes it possible to approach the uncanny figure of Silas and become reacquainted with that part of the self which has "become alienated only by the process of repression." Once recovered, that estranged aspect of the self becomes what Carroll calls "the irreducible core of human affection at the center of valid mythologies."[16]

[15] "The Uncanny," *Standard Edition,* XVII, 241.
[16] *"Silas Marner:* Reversing the Oracles of Religion," p. 200.

Three

Romola

George Eliot began her struggle with *Romola* shortly after the completion of *The Mill on the Floss*. She hoped that her trip to Rome would "chase away Maggie and the Mill"[1] from her thoughts, and this hope seems to have carried over to the conception of a new novel to be set in fifteenth-century Florence and centered on the life of Savonarola. What could be further from the sorrows of Maggie? The author looked forward to the project: "It will require a great deal of study and labor, and I am athirst to begin,"[2] she wrote to John Blackwood.

Research for the new novel was interrupted by the "sudden inspiration" for *Silas Marner,* and was then resumed with a second trip to Florence to gather more material. The original enthusiasm faded, however, when six months of poring over historical documents at home had failed to produce the beginning of a novel. At this point George Eliot felt "utterly despondent," "trying to

[1] *Letters,* III, 285.
[2] Ibid., p. 307.

write, trying to construct, and unable."[3] She was convinced that her difficulty stemmed from insufficient
historical knowledge, yet the more learning she acquired, the greater was her paralysis. Lewes, according to his
letter to Blackwood, saw her difficulty in a different
light:

Polly is still deep in her researches. Your presence will I hope
act like a stimulus to her to make her begin. At present she remains immovable in the conviction that she *can't* write the romance because she has not knowledge enough. Now as a
matter of fact I know that she has immensely more knowledge
of the particular period than any other writer who has touched
it; but her distressing diffidence paralyzes her.[4]

Lack of self-confidence was always with George Eliot,
but according to Lewes it was unusually debilitating at
this time, and was the primary obstacle to the writing
of *Romola,* as well as the source of her need to do mountains of research.

Lewes's interpretation, translated into my own
terms, points up a development of the utmost importance in understanding *Romola.* As I see it, the ending of
The Mill on the Floss constituted an alarming self-
confrontation for George Eliot, to which her initial
response was an overwhelmingly increased fear of impulse (recognized as an increase in her usual self-
distrust) and an equally intensified marshaling of defenses. The first of these defenses appears in the author's sudden determination to write an historical novel. But the life of Savonarola, a father-figure who is
ultimately executed, was too closely connected to the
feared impulses to function very well as a defense. The

[3] Quoted in Haight, p. 353.
[4] Ibid., p. 353.

intellectual activity involved in historical research, however, proved to be an overly adequate defense— it blocked creativity altogether.

As long as Savonarola remained the focus of George Eliot's efforts, she could not bring her research to an end and begin to write. Her situation resembled Schiller's description of blocked creativity:

It seems a bad thing and detrimental to the creative work of the mind if Reason makes too close an examination of the ideas as they come pouring in—at the very gateway, as it were. Looked at in isolation, a thought may seem very trivial or very fantastic; but it may be made important by another thought that comes after it, and, in conjunction with other thoughts that may seem equally absurd, it may turn out to form a most effective link. Reason cannot form any opinion upon all this unless it retains the thought long enough to look at it in connection with the others. On the other hand, where there is a creative mind, Reason—so it seems to me—relaxes its watch upon the gates, and the ideas rush in pell-mell, and only then does it look them through and examine them in a mass.[5]

Eventually, George Eliot shifted her focus from Savonarola to a heroine who could fulfill her defensive needs and at the same time function as an outlet for disguised fantasy. The name "Romola" first appeared in the author's journal on January 1, 1862 (a year and a half after the choice of subject), and three months later she had written seventy-seven pages and was at last "writing with pleasure."[6]

Interest in the heroine, once she appears, is impeded rather than fostered by the density of documentation

[5] Quoted by Freud in "The Method of Interpreting Dreams," *Standard Edition*, IV, 103.

[6] Rosemary Sprague, *George Eliot: A Biography* (New York, 1968), p. 204.

which goes so far beyond providing the necessary "medium" that it becomes a distraction if not an insurmountable obstacle to the reader. Throughout the novel there is an infuriating quantity of historical detail which almost seems to be designed to prevent that "special relaxation into the mental set appropriate to fiction."[7] We are definitely not invited, as we are in *The Mill on the Floss*, to submerge ourselves in dreamy visions. As Carole Robinson observes, in *Romola* George Eliot is making a "strenuous effort at affirmation," and in so doing she creates "not so much a novel as an essay in uncertainties."[8] The novel's highly charged imagery seems to lead nowhere and belong to no one (or at least not to Romola), while the heroine's search for moral absolutes is belabored in isolation.

It is possible, however, to piece together the fantasy content beneath the "essay in uncertainties," and to relate the unconscious needs and fears we uncover to the conscious preoccupations of the work. If we take the idealized heroine as our starting point, a contrast with Maggie emerges which indicates by omission what the author is trying to avoid.

Romola is presented as an intelligent and ardent young woman who progresses from a narrow life of personal emotional ties to a broader life of commitment to humanity. Her development has three stages. At first the meaning of life for her depends totally on devotion to her father, Bardo, a blind humanist scholar. This devotion, as a raison d'être, is challenged on the

[7] Norman N. Holland, *The Dynamics of Literary Response* (New York, 1968), p. 68.
[8] "*Romola*: A Reading of the Novel," *Victorian Studies* 6 (September 1962): 30-31.

one hand by Tito, who represents sensual egotism,[9] and on the other hand by the brief reappearance of her brother, Dino, who represents spiritual egotism. But Romola's devotion to duty is unwavering until a moral vacuum is created by the death of her father and the betrayal of his last wish by her husband. The second stage of her development begins when her flight from Tito and Florence is interrupted by Savonarola, who offers a new concept of devotion to humanity and becomes a substitute for the dead father. When Savonarola refuses to save Romola's godfather from execution, this second moral system collapses and Romola again runs away. The third stage begins when she sets out to sea in order to let destiny decide whether or not to end her life. She wakes up to the dire necessities of a plague-stricken village and a new commitment so absolute that it requires no thought, no decision, and no external guide.

It may seem surprising that, in this novel so carefully aimed at avoiding another personal history, we are presented (after considerable hesitation, of course) with a central character whose situation is even closer, in some respects, to the author's own life than Maggie's had been. Romola's devotion to her aged father parallels those years of Marian Evans's life, from sixteen to thirty, that were devoted to the care of her aging father. The Romola-Bardo relationship has the same Oedipal overtones as the father-daughter relationships in *Silas Marner* and *The Mill on the Floss*. But again, as in the portrayal of Maggie, we find that Oedipal desires are not the primary focus of defensive efforts. Love for the father is easily idealized, and thus made acceptable

9 Ibid., 36.

as a moral principle. The idealization transforms Oedipal love into a defense against resentment and rage.

One of the first things we have to notice about Romola's relationship to her father is her lack of resentment. When we are introduced to her, she is patiently waiting on Bardo, devoting herself completely to his needs and desires. In return, he complains of being abandoned by his son, and abuses Romola for being an inadequate "coadjutor" to him.[10] In his words, "the sustained zeal and unconquerable patience demanded from those who would tread the unbeaten paths of knowledge are still less reconcilable with the wandering, vagrant propensity of the feminine mind than with the feeble powers of the feminine body" (I, v, 75).

Under such treatment, the intensity of Romola's devotion becomes a sure sign that conflicting feelings are being repressed. In *The Mill on the Floss* the father also downgrades female capacities. And with far less provocation than Romola is given, Maggie's resentment eventually emerges in "fits of anger and hatred" toward everyone she loves (IV, iii). Her anger and hatred frighten her and give rise to defenses. But Romola's resentment never emerges. She is idealized by the removal (splitting off) of feared impulses, and by the glorification of her devotion, which is approved. She may be nearly as limited in her responses as Silas Marner in his reduced character, but her limitations are offered as virtues.

The appearance of such a simplified character, after the achieved complexity of Maggie, implies that in Maggie the author had seen more than she could cope

10 George Eliot, *Romola*, Warwickshire Edition (New York, 1907), vol. I, chap. v, p. 75. Subsequent references are to this edition.

with. If this is the case, it is relevant to note that Romola's moral quest is a highly extended version of the mental struggle that interrupts and breaks off Maggie's elopement with Stephen Guest. But the underlying conflict between id and superego which was discernible in Maggie's case has, in Romola's quest, been intellectualized into a conflict within the superego between various kinds of duties.

The urgency of Romola's need for some compelling duty is a measure of the fearsome strength of the impulses that must be warded off. We begin to see what these impulses are when we turn to the character of Tito. He is essentially as simplified a character as Romola, but of a different moral cast. His naive hedonism, in which the "end of life" is "but to extract the utmost sum of pleasure" (I, xi, 170), is perhaps unlikely for a man of such extensive education as Tito is set up to be. But his sensuality is quite convincing. He has the air "of a fleet, soft-coated, dark eyed animal . . . that unexpectedly pillows its chin on your palm, and looks up at you desiring to be stroked—as if it loved you" (I, vi, 87). He considers Romola a "joy that was due to him and was close to his lips, which he felt he was not bound to thrust away from him and so travel on, thirsting" (I, xi, 171). He fears whatever might "rob him of his pleasure," but lacks that "terror of the unseen" which is "the initial recognition of a moral law restraining desire" (I, xi, 171-72).

Tito is thus defined as a moral contrast to Romola. But in their opposite treatment of strikingly similar fathers we begin to see the essential unity of the two characters. We meet Tito long before we meet Romola, but we learn nothing of his relationship with his foster-father until after we have seen Romola interacting with her father. Then, as an obvious contrast, we are told that Tito has abandoned his foster-father, that he has thought it a relief to be quit of him, and that "such thoughts spring inevitably out of a relation that is irksome" (I, ix, 148). Thus the doubt created by the exaggeration of Romola's devotion is strengthened when Tito supplies the missing negative feelings, and the two characters begin to look like opposing aspects of one psyche.

Both Romola and Tito are substitutes for the missing Dino. Romola's devotion to her father takes the form of attempting in every way possible to replace the son who abandoned Bardo to become a monk. She can think of marrying only in the context of this devotion: she would marry a scholar who had the ability to carry on her father's work as her brother was meant to do.[11] This is the role that Tito comes to fill. Both Romola and Bardo immediately see him as a substitute for Dino:

> Romola's astonishment could hardly have been greater if the stranger had worn a panther-skin and carried a thyrsus; for the cunning barber had said nothing of the Greek's age or appearance; and among her father's scholarly visitors, she had hardly ever seen but middle-aged or grey-headed men. There was only one masculine face, at once youthful and beautiful, the image of which remained deeply impressed on her mind: it was that of her brother, who long years ago had taken her on his knee, kissed her, and never come back again: a fair face, with sunny hair, like her own. (I, v, 86)

Soon Bardo is addressing Tito as "my son" (I, xii, 175). When he tells Tito of the son he lost, he concludes with emotion that he has "found a son again" in him.

[11] Note the parallel between this attitude toward marriage and Eppie's in *Silas Marner*.

This parallel again implies the oneness of Tito and Romola. It also sheds further light on the impulses that lie behind Romola's quest for moral absolutes. Dino is harshly critical of the father he abandoned. On his deathbed he explains his action to Romola:

"I have never repented fleeing from the stifling poison-breath of sin that was hot and thick around me, and threatened to steal over my senses like besotting wine. My father could not hear the voice that called me night and day; he knew nothing of the demon-tempters that tried to drag me back from following it. My father has lived amidst human sin and misery without believing in them: he has been like one busy picking shining stones in a mine, while there was a world dying of plague above him. I spoke, but he listened with scorn. I told him the studies he wished me to live for were either childish trifling— dead toys—or else they must be made warm and living by pulses that beat to worldly ambitions and fleshly lusts, for worldly ambitions and fleshly lusts made all the substance of the poetry and history he wanted me to bend my eyes on continually." (I, xv, 229)[12]

Romola's response is righteous indignation—no sense of any truth in Dino's view of their father, no sympathy for his individual needs, only intense belief that the father has led a "pure and noble life."

Dino's judgment of Bardo is discredited by its proximity to a vision which, we are told, came "from the shadowy region where human souls seek wisdom apart from the human sympathies which are the very life and substance of our wisdom" (I, xv, 238). Nevertheless, there is a great deal of truth in Dino's words. Bardo

[12] This passage foreshadows Dorothea's response to Rome in *Middlemarch,* and suggests to me how much is lost through the overly defensive idealization of Romola. Dorothea has the ardor and moral seriousness of her predecessor, but she can engage a reader more fully than Romola because her exaggerations are accompanied by suggestions of the psychic conflict they are part of.

openly takes pride in being cut off from the world around him:

"For me, Romola, even when I could see, it was with the great dead that I lived; while the living often seemed to me mere spectres—shadows dispossessed of true feeling and intelligence . . . I have returned from the converse of the streets as from a forgotten dream, and have sat down among my books, saying with Petrarca, the modern who is least unworthy to be named after the ancients, 'Libri medullitus delectant, colloquuntur, consulunt, et viva quadam nobis atque arguta familiaritate junguntur.' " (I, v, 74-75)

Bardo's pedantry and his preference for the "great dead" over the living help to justify Dino's rejection of the scholar's life, and also reveal that Bardo, too, sought wisdom "apart from the human sympathies."

In Dino's revulsion for "fleshly lusts," the "demon-tempters" that sought to drag him back, we are reminded of the demons fought by Maggie and Godfrey Cass. But in *Romola* the fear of sexuality as such is insignificant beside the more regressive fear of anal-sadistic rage. The most intense emotions in the novel are found in the foster-father abandoned by Tito—a character as far removed as possible from Romola. But Baldassarre is an exaggerated version of Romola's father, so that the oneness of the two fathers creates a link between Baldassarre's pure hate and Romola's pure love.

We meet Bardo first—an old man whose scholarly ambitions are unfulfilled, and whose hope of fulfilling them through his son has been frustrated and turned to fierce bitterness. He is exacting, impatient, suspicious, and unappreciative—qualities exacerbated by the blindness and age which have rendered him powerless. We see Bardo in action, and cannot help but remember him when Baldassarre is described thus:

Baldassarre was exacting, and had got stranger as he got older; he was constantly scrutinizing Tito's mind to see whether it answered to his own exaggerated expectations; and age—the age of a thick-set, heavy-browed, bald man beyond sixty, whose intensity and eagerness in the grasp of ideas have long taken the character of monotony and repetition, may be looked at from many points of view without being found attractive. (I, ix, 146)

Like Bardo, Baldassarre was a scholar, and one who saw his adopted son as the means of realizing his dreams of glory. In his description of the mental confusion that followed the shipwreck and separation from Tito, he identifies his son with his knowledge:

"And when I was in the ship on the waters I began to know what I longed for; it was for the Boy to come back—it was to find all my thoughts again, for I was locked away outside them all. And I am outside now. I feel nothing but a wall and darkness." (II, liii, 237)

The "wall and darkness" belong to a pattern of imagery which carries a sense of obstruction through the novel. For Bardo "blindness acts like a dam" against "the streams of thought" (I, v, 76). His son, Dino, was to provide "the sharp edge of a young mind to pierce the way," but without him the "path" has "closed in" and become a "narrow track." The image of dammed-up "streams of thought" is developed in Baldassarre's loss of "rare knowledge:"

It had all slipped away from him—that laboriously gathered store. Was it utterly and for ever gone from him, like the waters from an urn lost in the wide ocean? Or, was it still within him, imprisoned by some obstruction that might one day break asunder? (I, xxx, 395)

Baldassarre's knowledge is a lost treasure, like his gems, and like Silas Marner's gold. Whether "imprisoned" within or lost "like the waters from an urn in the wide ocean," the lost knowledge, like Silas's gold, has anal significance.[13]

Tito remembers life with Baldassarre as having "some of the stint and subjection of a school" and "it was a great relief" to him to be rid of the relationship. He tries to convince himself that Baldassarre is dead without recognizing it as a wish. In fact, his disguised hostility is emphatically limited to passive aggression. His abandonment of his father was passive: they were separated by external forces, and Tito simply declined to go in search of him. But his lack of "active malignity" becomes somewhat unbelievable when, after Baldassarre has tried to kill him, Tito forms no plan of retaliation. There seems to be special significance to repeated "set pieces"[14] like the following:

It was a characteristic fact in Tito's experience at this crisis that no direct measures for ridding himself of Baldassarre ever occurred to him. All other possibilities passed through his mind, even to his own flight from Florence; but he never thought of any scheme for removing his enemy. His dread generated no active malignity, and he would have been glad not to give pain to any mortal. (I, xxiii, 331)

Baldassarre, by contrast, is reduced to "a sort of mad consciousness that he was a solitary pulse of just rage

[13] Anality is also evident in Bardo's relationship to his knowledge, but it is more subtly conveyed and prefigures the fuller characterization of Casaubon in *Middlemarch*.

[14] In *The Novels of George Eliot* (New York and London, 1959) Jerome Thale finds that in *Romola* George Eliot "elevates psychology to a major concern—and overtaxes her resources." The strain is evident not because her psychological analysis is not "integrated with the general narrative" but "presented as set psychological pieces." (Pp. 80-81.) I would attribute the lack of integration to overdefensiveness, which puts rigid limits on the psychological analysis.

(II, xxxiv, 28). His hatred has "the indestructible independent force of a supreme emotion, which knows no terror, and asks for no motive, which is itself an ever-burning motive, consuming all other desire" (II, xxxviii, 71).

The insistence on Tito's lack of "active malignity," and the absoluteness of it in Baldassarre, are extremes which suggest that another defense has been added to the splitting—a kind of reversal intended to remove the anal rage as far as possible from the center of the novel. Not only has hostility toward the father been projected onto a secondary child and father outside the central pair (Romola-Bardo), but also the roles have been reversed, so that it is the foster-father who is actively trying to kill the child (and finally succeeds).

The descriptions of Baldassarre's moments of recovered memory provide a vivid confirmation of the psychoanalytic theory of the influence of anality on the thinking processes in compulsion neurosis. Baldassarre, after rejecting Tito's apology and breaking his dagger against his enemy's armor, suddenly recovers his ability to read. The Greek letters, which had been as meaningless as water marks, are transformed into "magic signs to conjure up a world." He "felt the glow of conscious power," and looking down at the mountains and valleys, the city and the river, he "felt himself master of them all." His "limbs recovered their strength" and "he was once more a man who knew cities, whose sense of vision was instructed with large experience, and who felt the keen delight of holding all things in the grasp of language. Names! Images!—his mind rushed through his wealth without pausing, like one who enters on a great inheritance" (II, xxxviii, 67-71).

The passage is a perfect example of thinking which, in Fenichel's terms, is permeated with "the archaic attitudes that accompanied the first use of words."[15] Words, at the anal stage, are possessions, mastered by the ego; to the adult who is retreating from the phallic Oedipus complex to anal sadism, words are both anal treasure and phallic potency.

The regression to anality which thus affects the thinking processes also affects the superego. When Baldassarre first formed his thoughts of revenge against Tito he reviewed all the disappointments of his life and thought: "this world is a lie—there is no goodness but hate" (I, xxx, 400). His paralyzed mind was first partly revived by Savonarola's "threatening voice" saying "The day of vengeance is at hand!" (I, xxv, 334). When his limbs became strong enough to kill, he thanked "the justice that struggled in this confused world in behalf of vengeance" (I, xxx, 401). Finally his precious words come back, released when a "sudden rage had shaken away the obstruction which stifled his soul." His hatred becomes "an ever burning motive"—the one principle of life. His "exquisite vengeance" will triumph over baseness (II, xxxviii, 69-71).

Thus the superego succumbs to the "regressive pull toward sadism" and takes on "archaic features"—notably, the talion principle.[16]

The usefulness of this analysis of Baldassarre's anality will, I think, justify its presence shortly. It seems to me that just as Baldassarre's "obstruction" is removed by a "sudden rage," so George Eliot's obstruction—

[15] Otto Fenichel, *The Psychoanalytic Theory of Neurosis* (New York, 1945), p. 295.
[16] Ibid., p. 291.

repression—is being removed by creating Baldassarre
and his rage. Baldassarre's anality helps us to unravel
the defensive fragmentation in the novel, and to see the
connection between the pervasive anal imagery and the
intellectualized weighing and measuring of duties that
dominates the Romola story. The feared impulse that is
chiefly being warded off in the idealized conception of
Romola is to be found in Baldassarre's anal rage. In
relation to Romola, anal rage would be a regressive
reponse to Oedipal frustration (one notices the conspicuous number of father-figures in the novel and the
equally significant fact that all of them die).[17] But
Romola seems to be created in accordance with the
author's superego demands as well as from a desire to
preserve an integration based on the father-daughter
relationship. Hence her devotion to the father (or
father-substitute), which is both Oedipal and oral-
dependent, is rationalized as duty. And because of its
origin in unresolved instinctual conflict, duty becomes
an obsessive concern.

The cumulative effect of the novel as a reflection of
the author's state of mind can also be elucidated in terms
of anal-compulsive thinking. As Carole Robinson aptly
puts it, "philosophic uncertainty is the keynote of the
novel, and the source of Romola's failure is to be sought
not in its moral intentions or its didacticism, but in
doubt, and in the novelist's uncertain faith in the
affirmations she proposes in her effort to satisfy
doubt."[18] This is a richly suggestive statement in the
context I have been setting up. The laboriousness with
which every phase and aspect of duty are explored in

[17] Robinson, "Romola: A Reading of the Novel," p. 40.
[18] Ibid., p. 31.

Romola qualifies as obsessive. And obsessive doubt is one characteristic of anal-compulsive thinking. "Doubt," to quote Fenichel again, "is the instinctual conflict displaced to the intellectual field."[19] It involves a "retreat from feeling to thinking" which usually fails, since the feelings that are being avoided—conflicts of masculinity versus femininity, love versus hate, id versus superego—become the unconscious content of obsessive doubts.

Thus, in spite of the defensive removal that a historical subject seems to provide, the historical moment chosen begins with the death of Lorenzo de' Medici and ends with the death of Savonarola. The disorder wrought by the deaths of these father-figures becomes the context for Romola's moral quest, and the unconscious conflict of love versus hate for the father is not successfully avoided. The quest itself, which is the center of the manifest content, becomes a vehicle for avoiding the latent emotional conflict by assuming the form of intellectual analysis rather than "showing."[20]

We are shown Romola's devotion to her father, but, as Levine notes, her "pride and rebelliousness are asserted far more than they are created."[21] She has a "strong impulse" to rebel against Tito, but the impulse is doubted as soon as she thinks about breaking the marriage tie. At this point Romola submits to Savonarola's guidance, and her act is presented as a moral contrast to the simultaneous triumph of Tito over his "lonely disowned" foster-father. He is saying "my father is dead" (II, xl, 102), while Romola is accepting

[19] Fenichel, p. 297.
[20] See George Levine, "*Romola* as Fable," in *Critical Essays on George Eliot,* ed. Hardy, p. 78.
[21] Ibid., p. 84.

Savonarola as "My father" (II, xxxix, 91). But the moral implication and the exaltation of Romola's "new fellowship with suffering" remain unconvincing abstractions.[22] Beneath the moral, lies the fear of impulse which has come to mean parricide. Duty is the only safeguard. If Romola ceases to love even Tito, she breaks a tie and opens up the horrible possibilities of rebellion:

The great need of her heart compelled her to strangle, with desperate resolution, every rising impulse of suspicion, pride, and resentment; she felt equal to any self-infliction that would save her from ceasing to love. That would be like the hideous nightmare in which the world had seemed to break away all round her, and leave her feet overhanging the darkness. (I, xxvii, 365)

Thus Romola's "trust in Savonarola is something like a rope suspended securely by her path" (II, xliv, 148), and her "works of womanly sympathy" give her a "firm footing" (II, xliv, 146). She brings to such works "the inspiration of her deepest feelings"—not so much the

[22] Robinson, p. 39. "The hollowness of George Eliot's praise of the life to which she has committed her heroine, the hollowness of the heroine herself, come not from the moral intention behind the novel, but from the novelist's uncertainty of the validity of that intention: 'And the inspiring consciousness breathed into her by Savonarola's influence that her lot was vitally united with the general lot had exalted even the minor details of obligation into religion. She was marching with a great army; she was feeling the stress of a common life. If victims were needed, and it was uncertain on whom the lot might fall, she would stand ready to answer to her name' (ch. lvi). The word 'stress' itself belies the pretended exaltation in a 'common life'; and 'victim' is an unfortunate epithet for a heroine of the people. George Eliot stands on the verge of a real conflict and problem of the modern novel here, the conflict between the individual and the organized state. But in her anxiety to affirm a basis for existence for her by now almost desperate heroine, she must avoid dealing with Romola's dissatisfaction."

claimed sympathy, however, as her fear of the "hideous nightmare" of impulse.

Tending the sick and feeding the hungry are ways of transforming love into duty—of putting love under the control of the superego.[23] Regressive anality is only apparent in the sadism of the superego which is directed inward and demands self-deprivation and willingness to make the self a victim. Love also regresses to its oral forms. Through submission to Savonarola Romola enters a "state of yearning passivity" and feels herself part of "something unspeakably great" (II, xli, 111-12; cf. Maggie and Dorothea). In his teaching she finds "immediate satisfaction for moral needs" which had been "left hungering" since her father's death. Her new "reason for living . . . seemed to need feeding with greater forces than she possessed within herself," and that "feeding" comes from her new guide, "a strong being who roused a new strength within herself" (II, xl, 111).

Any real "showing" of this stage in Romola's life would be apt to reveal too clearly actual distaste for tending the sick, the constant effort involved in identifying herself with the common people, and the uncon-

[23] Rebellion has on its side the instinctual impulse—anal-sadistic rage against the father—and the sadistic severity of the superego which demands absolutes. Duty that is less than perfect (or a guide who is less than perfect) must be rejected, rebelled against, because only a perfect duty can ward off emerging hate. Submission has on its side the superego's dependence on duty, and also the instinctual need for love. The natural love for the father is the primary obstacle to hate. But when that love becomes Oedipal and is both forbidden and frustrated, it must undergo a number of transformations in order to continue to ward off hate. On the one hand love is taken up by the superego and made into a duty, and on the other it takes regressive forms, both oral and anal.

scious needs and fears behind the effort. Thus her role
as "Madonna" to the sick and hungry Florentines is not
adequately realized in the novel. We actually see her
tending only once sick man. He happens to be Tito's
abandoned foster-father, and all of the impact of the
passage falls on the identity of the man, rather than on
Romola's feelings about her "works of womanly sympathy." We hear more adoring praise of her and more
descriptions of her "sublime excitement" than her actions can support. Her severly limited moral and emotional state is treated as though it were great and noble,
and the reader is unconvinced.

Romola's new reason for living becomes very precarious when she begins to have serious doubts about
Savonarola. Just as her sense of some defect in her
devotedness to her father increased her need to fulfill
his last wishes, and her misgivings about Tito increased
her determination to love him, so Romola's doubts
about Savonarola (with the help of his excommunica-
tion) increase her attachment to and dependence on
him. Awareness of his faults "made all life look ghastly
to her," so she doubles her efforts to see him in a
"simplified and ennobled" light (II, lv, 249). But when
Savonarola refuses to rescue her godfather from execution, Romola once again runs away from Florence. "A
new rebellion had risen within her," and she "despaired
of finding any consistent duty" (II, lxi, 311).

Duty, in *Romola,* is a means of reconciling the superego
to the disguised indulgence of oral and Oedipal wishes as
well as a means of warding off rage. The equilibrium of
this arrangement is precarious because the father-
figure's role is idealized and the superego is severe in
proportion to the resentment that is being repressed.

Thus when Savonarola fails to live up to his idealized role, the whole duty system collapses. And without it Romola seems to lose her identity: "Why should she care about wearing one badge more than another, or being called by her own name?" (II, lxi, 311).

Romola's sadistic superego, directed against herself, has been the mainstay of her identity up to this point.[24] We have seen the same kind of superego functioning in Maggie, but with less stable control, and will see it again in Dorothea. But in neither of these other characters is the effort to "strangle . . . every rising impulse" (I, xxvii, 365) as desperate and consistent as it is in Romola, whose most memorable quality is "marble" erectness.[25] Her superego demands "strangle" with the same ferocity as the opposite forces in Tito, which "alter his face, as a face is altered by a hidden muscular tension with which a man is secretly throttling or stamping out the life from something feeble, yet dangerous" (II, xlviii, 181).

Thus when Romola's superego system collapses, she runs away not so much from an external situation as from an intolerable inner tension which now can be

[24] Karen Horney's description of the kind of ideal self which develops out of the "self-effacing solution" is an aid to understanding this specialized identity. See *Neurosis and Human Growth* (New York, 1950), pp. 214-38.

[25] Romola's "marble" quality suggests that, like Tito, she has her armor. Tito's actual armor, "the garment of fear" (I, xxvi, 349), is frightening to Romola, as if a fiend had changed his "sensitive human skin into a hard shell" (I, xxvii, 370). But like her father's armor—"My armour is the *aes triplex* of a clear conscience, and a mind nourished by the precepts of philosophy" (I, v, 83)—Romola's has behind it the fear which is a barrier between thought and feeling. The pervasive imagery of obstruction and piercing in the novel reflects the prominence of fears and defenses in the author's state of mind.

relieved only by a further regression. The anal-sadistic equilibrium gives way to a passive oral-receptive mode.[26]

Romola takes flight from Florence to the sea, and from the intense effort of endless inner argument to thoughts of "gliding over the waters" (II, lxi, 314). She "longed for that repose in mere sensation which she had sometimes dreamed of in the sultry afternoons of her early girlhood, when she had fancied herself floating naiad-like in the waters." The state she longs for is like Maggie's "dreamy gliding," but Romola's indulgence of this longing will apparently hurt no one— except possibly herself.

When Romola passively abandons herself to the sea, she is longing for parents, and dreams of seeking the beloved dead in the tomb. She feels "orphaned in those wide spaces of sea and sky" (II, lxi, 317). When she wakes from her night on the sea, she seems to find a mother in nature. Her boat is "lying still in a little creek" beside "a deep curve of the mountains," a "crescent-shaped nook" that has the shape and sheltering qualities of a mother's body. Here in the "deep curve," "the delicious sun-rays fell on Romola and thrilled her gently like a caress":

She lay motionless, hardly watching the scene; rather, feeling simply the presence of peace and beauty. While we are still in our youth there can always come, in our early waking, moments when mere passive existence is itself a Lethe, when the exquisiteness of subtle indefinite sensation creates a bliss which is without memory and without desire. (II, lxviii, 385)

[26] Fenichel, pp. 369-70. Impulsive running away involves "regression toward passive-receptive forms of mastery," and is an attempt to reach a place which means a "helping oral mother" and "gratification without guilt." "In a symbolic way, this pursuit of rest and of protection at the mother's breast is expressed in the frequent yearning for the boundless ocean . . . "

When Romola drifts out to sea, the setting not only changes from city to country, but from realistic-historical to openly symbolic.[27] The sea is the water of birth, and the landing place is the mother. Maggie was borne on the waters and drowned, but Romola is borne along to a mother-like refuge—an easy birth. The primal state of blissful oneness remains "untroubled" only for a few moments. As soon as Romola realizes that her boat has become "the gently lulling cradle of a new life," she hears the cry of a hungry baby which "no one came to help" (II, lxviii, 386). She is "irresistibly" drawn to it, and finds that the baby's parents have died of the plague.

At this point the regression undergoes a reversal so that it is not Romola who is being mothered, but Romola who is mothering. Nevertheless, in the scenes which follow, her actual ministrations to the sick villagers and the orphaned Benedetto are described in much less detail than the passive period of rest she enjoys after everyone is well again:

> She had taken for her dwelling one of the houses abandoned by their owners, standing a little aloof from the village street; and here on a thick heap of clean straw—a delicious bed for those who do not dream of down—she felt glad to lie still through most of the daylight hours, taken care of along with the little Benedetto by a woman whom the pestilence had widowed. (II, lxviii, 397)

The villagers not only visit the "blessed lady" (when they ask "Who are you?" she answers,"I came over the sea . . . "); they also feed her "honey, fresh cakes, eggs, and polenta" (II, lxviii, 391, 397). In such details we can

---

[27] See Levine, "*Romola* as Fable," p. 96.

see, despite the reversal, the underlying wish to be nurtured by a mother.

Romola's return to Florence is an extension of this regression, with its reversal to mothering. Her decision to go back is described in terms of hunger and feeding:

Florence, and all her life there, had come back to her like hunger; her feelings could not go wandering after the possible and the vague: their living fibre was fed with the memory of familiar things. (II, lxix, 400)

Upon her return, Romola goes to great lengths to find Tessa and Tito's children. We are told that she "never for a moment told herself that it was heroism or exalted charity in her to seek these beings," but the implication is that Romola's action *was* heroic and exalted. Much more convincing is this comment: "she needed something that she was bound specially to care for; she yearned to clasp the children and to make them love her" (II, lxx, 406). The urgency of this last statement is a clue to the relative importance of heroism versus personal need in her motivation.

There is a slight shock produced by the abrupt switch to a symbolic landscape at the beginning of Romola's regression, but the orality itself does not come as a surprise. Beside the preponderant anal imagery in the earlier parts of the novel, there is a less emphatic oral pattern. For example, early in the story, Romola is described as "simple and unreserved as a child in her love for Tito" (I, xvii, 260). Later on she recalls that love in terms reminiscent of the oral merging sought by Maggie:

Romola was carried, by a sudden wave of memory, back again into the time of perfect trust, and felt again the presence of the husband whose love made the world as fresh and wonderful to her as to a little child that sits in stillness among the sunny flowers: heard the gentle tones and saw the soft eyes without any lie in them, and breathed again that large freedom of the soul which comes from the faith that the being who is nearest us is greater than ourselves. And in those brief moments the tears always rose; the woman's lovingness felt something akin to what the bereaved mother feels when the tiny fingers seem to lie warm on her bosom, and yet are marble to her lips as she bends over the silent bed. (II, xxxvi, 44-45)

Like Maggie's memory of childhood bliss with Tom, Romola's memory of "eyes without any lie in them" is an illusion. There were lies between Tito and Romola from the beginning. The illusion is created by the longing for a "time of perfect trust" which the infant experiences at the mother's breast, as the final image in this passage reveals. The turn at the end, in which Romola is not the "little child" but the bereaved mother, makes the same reversal that we see in the birth episode.

The same kind if imagery is often used to describe Tito, especially in his relationship with Tessa. To begin with, the shipwrecked Tito is hungry and finds the "poor child" asleep by her wooden milk vessels. She feeds him and later becomes a refuge for him. At the same time, Tito acts as her protector and parent. He relives with Tessa his earliest memories of rescue and "sweet food and soothing caresses" (I, ix, 146). Whenever he rescues her from some danger, he also feeds her and notices her baby features and childlike innocence (I, x, 152). When he encounters Tessa in church, after he has become entangled in deceits, he sees her as "a large image of a sweet sleepy child" and at the same time as a refuge:

Tito felt an irresistible desire to go up to her and get her pretty trusting looks and prattle: this creature who was without moral judgment that could condemn him, whose little loving ignorant soul made a world apart, where he might feel in freedom from suspicions and exacting demands, had a new attraction for him now. She seemed a refuge from the threatened isolation that would come with disgrace. (I, xiv, 217)

He finally sets up a home which will be an "inviting refuge" for himself and where Tessa can sit in "happy passiveness" with her baby (II, xxiv, 21).

Tessa is ostensibly a mother, but essentially she is a child who embodies Romola's need to cling (II, liii, 231) and her desire for "repose in mere sensation." The first time we see her she is enjoying just such repose as she stands sleeping by her milk vessels. When Romola returns lost Lillo to his home she finds Tessa asleep by the cradle she had been rocking. And at the end of the novel she is still the same sleepy child, but united with Romola:

Her rounded face wore even a more perfect look of childish content than in her young days: everybody was so good in the world, Tessa thought; even Monna Brigida never found fault with her now, and did little else than sleep, which was an amiable practice in everybody, and one that Tessa liked for herself. (II, Epilogue, 427)

The negative aspect of oral dependency is also apparent in the "foolish and helpless" Tessa. Romola thinks of her as "this poor, trusting, ignorant thing, with the child's mind in the woman's body" (II, lvi, 259), who cannot survive without a parent any more than the orphaned Benedetto could. At one point she is rescued by Romola:

It was like a change in a dream to Tessa—the escape from nightmare into floating safety and joy—to find herself taken care of by this lady, so lovely and powerful and gentle. She let

Romola unfasten her necklace and clasp, while she herself did nothing but look up at the face that bent over her. (I, l, 210)

In this rescue Romola takes over Tito's protective role, but in her later flight to the sea she repeats Tessa's "escape from nightmare into floating safety and joy." The reversal to mothering, which interrupts Romola's regressive bliss, seems to be a means of avoiding the helplessness of Tessa.

This reversal is a tidy way to balance oral needs and fears, and to reconcile them with superego demands. Romola becomes a combined mother-father to Tessa and her children and thus, like Silas Marner, participates vicariously in the fulfillment of the child's longing for parents. But for Romola the reversal also involves a reassertion of the claims of the past and the superego. At one point in her regression she feels as completely cut off as Silas did in migrating to Raveloe. But her isolated self-confrontation is not allowed to develop. While she rests from her labors in the plague-stricken village, Romola's mind is filled with "self-reproach" (she had too easily "lost all her trust" II, lxix, 399-401) and with thoughts of the past. Her new sense of her own needs and her longing for "familiar things" unite as a new superego demand patterned after the old.

This process may seem to recapitulate and even go beyond Silas Marner's regeneration. But it is all stated rather than shown. What is truly "shown" is not Romola's self-confrontation and reintegration, but the confrontation between Tito and Baldassarre, in which the hostility toward the father is acted out. When Savonarola's death is added to theirs, fathers and brothers have been completely eliminated and both Oedipal and sadistic dangers avoided. Thus while *Silas*

Marner begins with regression and moves toward a basically Oedipal position combined with aspects of oral dependency, *Romola* moves toward a regressive orality and away from the Oedipal conflict and its anal-sadistic resolution. It leaves us with a sense not so much of rebirth and reconciliation, but of something closer to Baldassarre's struggling in the waters, trying to "get a firm grasp somewhere, and lift himself above these waters that floated over him" (I, xxx, 405). The affirmation in *Romola* is like the "pretty loving apparition" of Tessa to Baldassarre—no more "than a faint rainbow on the blackness to the man who is wrestling in deep waters" (II, xxxiii, 11).

Four

Felix Holt

Although often classed with *Romola* as another of George
Eliot's stiff, over-intellectualized works, *Felix Holt, the
Radical* reflects a more open and balanced state of mind. It
is true that, once again, the author's scrupulous research
(this time political, economic, and legal) produces details
which obstruct the movement of the novel. She still
seems unable to let the story develop freely out of the
qualities and interactions of her characters.[1] But her
intense resistance to the impulses revealed in Maggie
seems to have reached and passed its peak in *Romola*.

---

[1] When *Felix Holt* first appeared in print a critic in the *Saturday Review*,
June 16, 1866, wrote: "It is a pity that the plot of the story happens to
flow from utterly remote and far off incidents, instead of flowing from
the mental movements of the principal actors." Quoted in John Holmstrom and Laurence Lerner, eds., *George Eliot and Her Readers* (New York,
1966), p. 70. Most subsequent criticism voices the same objection.
Arnold Kettle argues that the "legal niceties, unexpected inheritances
and complex intrigues" are means of dispensing with the "political and
moral problems set in motion in the novel" which the author is incapable of working through to completion. *"Felix Holt, the Radical,"* in
Critical Essays on George Eliot, ed. Barbara Hardy (New York, 1970), p. 107.

With *The Spanish Gypsy*, a tragic drama in verse which
was to succeed *Romola*, George Eliot again experienced
despair and blocked creativity. The drama was to have
the grandeur of Greek tragedy and reflect the impact of
"foregoing hereditary conditions" on an unsuspecting
young woman:

A young maiden, believing herself to be on the eve of the chief
event of her life—marriage—about to share in the ordinary lot
of womanhood, full of young hope, has suddenly announced to
her that she is chosen to fulfill a great destiny, entailing a
terribly different experience from that of ordinary womanhood.[2]

This projected drama of renunciation promises to touch
on the kind of conflict between duty and desire (mixed
with fear) portrayed in Maggie's renunciation of marri-
riage to Stephen Guest, and to create, as in *Romola*,
another absolute duty (based on a father's claim) as a
defense against desire. But George Eliot's work brought
her to a "horrible scepticism" which paralyzed her mind
as her work on *Romola* had done.[3] Finally she set the
unfinished drama aside to write another English story
that had been on her mind.

Felix Holt was not a "sudden inspiration" thrusting
itself before the Spanish drama as *Silas Marner* did with
Romola. But the novel provides evidence that, in
Schiller's terms, "Reason" was the beginning to relax its
watch upon the gates. The drama's theme of great
renunciation gave way to Esther's less dramatic renunciation of wealth and social status for the kind of marriage that belongs to "the ordinary lot of womanhood."
This shift alone suggests that some reconciliation be-

---

[2] Haight, p. 376, quoting the Notes to *The Spanish Gypsy*.
[3] Haight, p. 378, quoting from her journal, July 17, 1864.

tween duty and desire is being sought which will transcend Romola's initial (and untenable) integration based on the father, and also her final regressive solution based on mothering.[4]

The manifest content of *Felix Holt*, like that of *Romola*, strenuously promotes altruism—the path of duty. The polar opposites, egoist and altruist, reappear in the selfish Mrs. Transome and the self-renouncing Felix Holt. But the portrayal of Felix reveals a more critical view of heroic selflessness than that of Romola, while sympathetic understanding of Mrs. Transome replaces the revulsion apparent in the treatment of Tito. Esther is presented as a potential egotist who must have a "terrible vision" of loveless isolation and despair (through Mrs. Transome) before making a firm commitment to the altruistic ideal identified with Felix.

The main object of my interpretation of *Felix Holt* will be to show how Esther's development—in psychological terms—furthers the maturing process that began with *The Mill on the Floss*. At the beginning, Esther's world of interests is almost as limited (and anal) as Silas Marner's, and she, too, is cut off from the past. But unlike Silas (who finds that the past is forever dark) she learns her stepfather's secret of "passion and struggle" and confronts a "bad" mother in Mrs. Transome. The embrace between this symbolic mother-daughter pair is the emotional climax of the novel and a key to understanding its achievements and its weaknesses.

Part I, below, discusses the initial characterization of

[4] It is altogether possible that the novel was first conceived as Mrs. Transome's tragedy, to which Felix Holt and the political theme were later added. See Fred C. Thomson, "The Genesis of *Felix Holt*," *PMLA* 74 (1959): 576-84.

Esther and the two contacts that impel her change—
Felix Holt and the secret of Rufus Lyon. Part II shifts to
the author's treatment of these two men and relates
Harold Transome's father-confrontation to the removal of the titular hero. Part III returns to Esther and the
significance of her "terrible vision" and mothering of
Mrs. Transome.

I

The story of Esther Lyon, although it is not the center of
emotional intensity, provides the novel with a beginning, middle, and end. At the outset her situation recalls
the father-daughter relationships of the earlier novels (a
clue to her significance for the author). But Esther is a
heroine strikingly different from her predecessors. She
is not the ideal daughter, devoted to her father, nor is she
devoted to "works of womanly sympathy" amid famine
and plague. In her world we return to the mudane
problems and mundane people that surrounded Maggie.

At the completion of her education abroad, Esther
chose to live at home with her father in preference to
serving as a governess in a well-born, wealthy family.
"But she was not contented with her life: she seemed to
herself to be surrounded with ignoble, uninteresting
conditions, from which there was no issue . . ."[5] Yet
Esther does not frighten herself with fits of anger and
frustration against her father and his mundane world
as Maggie did. She is content with herself, and assumes
her superiority to everyone around her:

She had one of those exceptional organizations which are
quick and sensitive without being in the least morbid; she was

[5] George Eliot, *Felix Holt, the Radical,* Warwickshire Edition (New
York, 1907), vol. I, chap. 6, p. 110. Subsequent references are to this
edition.

alive to the finest shades of manner, to the nicest distinctions of tone and accent; she had a little code of her own about scents and colours, textures and behaviour, by which she secretly condemned or sanctioned all things and persons. And she was well satisfied with herself for her fastidious taste, never doubting that hers was the highest standard. She was proud that the best-born and handsomest girls at school had always said that she might be taken for a born lady . . . and she felt that it was her superiority which made her unable to use without disgust any but the finest cambric handkerchiefs and the freshest gloves. (I, 6, 110)

Like Maggie, Esther dreams of being a queen, but her daydreams involve no transformation of herself, only transformation of her surroundings into more suitable elegance.

Esther's affection for her father is limited by her tastes and by her general lack of empathy. She "recognized the purity of his character, and a quickness of intellect in him which responded to her own liveliness, in spite of what seemed a dreary piety, which selected everything that was least interesting and romantic in life and history" (I, 6, 112). If she knew that her father had a want, she would "supply it with some pretty device of a surprise." But she is neither very aware of his personal wants, nor motivated to gratify his greatest want "of seeing her under convictions, and fit to become a member of the church." She is able to spend all of her earnings gratifying her "nice tastes," feeling sure, at the same time, that she is "generous" (I, 6, 111). And her father finds himself "in timorous subjection to her wishes."

Such a heroine is as much of a surprise to a reader who has just come away from the grave, upright Romola, as Esther is to the equally serious Felix Holt, through whose eyes we first see her:

The minister's daughter was not the sort of person he expected. She was quite incongruous with his notion of ministers' daughters in general; and though he had expected something nowise delightful, the incongruity repelled him. A very delicate scent, the faint suggestion of a garden, was wafted as she went. He would not observe her, but he had a sense of an elastic walk, the tread of small feet, a long neck and a high crown of shining brown plaits with curls that floated backward—things, in short, that suggested a fine lady to him, and determined him to notice her as little as possible. (I, 5, 96)

Esther irreverently takes advantage of Lyon's lengthy blessing before tea to observe Felix Holt, in whom she sees "a peculiar looking person, but not insignificant, which was the quality that most hopelessly consigned a man to perdition" (I, 5, 97). When Felix upsets her frilled workbasket and discovers her volume of Byron, Esther shows spirit in defending herself and Byron, and sauciness in mocking Felix's ferocity. The mockery is deserved, but Felix's judgment of Esther is nevertheless largely shared by the narrator, who comments a bit wryly that Esther's sauciness "was always charming because it was without emphasis, and was accompanied with graceful little turns of the head." This kind of charm aligns Esther with Tito, and her criticism of Miss Jermyn as "vulgarity personified—with large feet, and the most odious scent on her handkerchief, and a bonnet that looks like 'The Fashion' printed in capital letters," again underlines her dissimilarity to the modest Romola, who had no interest in the world of ladies and fashion and would never mock anyone.

The introductory portrayal of Esther's character, which puts so much emphasis on her self-satisfaction, ends on a different note—a feeling "that she should have loved her mother better than she was able to love her father," and a wish to remember her mother that is close to longing:

But she had no more than a broken vision of the time before she was five years old—the time when the word oftenest on her lips was "Mamma"; when a low voice spoke caressing French words to her, and she in her turn repeated the words to her rag-doll; when a very small white hand, different from any that came after used to pat her, and stroke her, and tie on her frock and pinafore, and when at last there was nothing but sitting with a doll on a bed where mamma was lying, till her father once carried her away. Where distinct memory began, there was no longer the low caressing voice and the small white hand. (I, 6, 112-13)

Esther's "broken vision" of her mother promises to give us a deeper understanding of the limitations and possibilities of her character than anything previous.

At this point the narrative suddenly shifts in mid-chapter from Esther to a flashback of Rufus Lyon's relationship with her mother (see below, pp. 114, 117-119). The oral nurturing in this account of a past romance foreshadows the relationship that will develop between Esther and Mrs. Transome, and the fact that the author interrupts the portrayal of Esther just as it begins to have some depth in relation to a lost mother provides a clue to the latent significance of Esther's development. The interruption also reveals the author's hesitancy in approaching directly the painful loss that underlies the orality in all of Esther's predecessors.

Following the flashback, the narrative returns to its former pattern. Esther's moral development begins with Felix Holt, through whom for the first time in her life she is "seriously shaken in her self-contentment" (I, 10, 182). Before this happens she has "begun to find him amusing, and also rather irritating to her woman's love of conquest. He always opposed and criticized her; and besides that, he looked at her as if he never saw a single detail about her person—quite as if she were a middle-aged woman in a cap." (I, 10, 173.) Esther's sexual attraction to Felix, subtly conveyed through her irritation (like Maggie's early treatment of Stephen Guest), gives him the power to influence her. The more directly he attacks her, the more resentful yet interested she becomes. When he finally cares enough to say "I want you to change," Esther is mortified. But through her wounded vanity "there pierced a sense that this exasperation of Felix against her was more complimentary than anything in his previous behaviour" (I, 10, 178). He raises in her mind a "strange contradiction of impulses" which leaves her in a "new kind of subjection" to someone who sees her as "trivial, narrow, and selfish" (I, 6, 181-82).

The fusion of moral awakening with sexual awakening is convincing at this point. Esther's inner tumult involves no denial of sexuality, even though she is not altogether as aware of the nature of her feelings as we are meant to be. But there is something disconcerting in the way Esther's "new consciousness concerning her father"—a result of Felix's criticism—leads to "spontaneous tenderness."

Esther up to this point is rarely warm or affectionate. Her senses, her emotions, and her judgments seem to be very narrowly bound up in substitutes for and defenses against sexual curiosity. She is first presented in the novel through the sense of smell. Her presence in the household is symbolized by the scent of dried rose leaves and wax candles, delicate scents quite "incongruous with the general air of sombreness and privation" in the Lyon home. The wax candles, paid for by Esther's earnings, are not a delicacy toward her father but toward herself. As Mr. Lyon apologetically explains to Felix Holt, she is "so delicately framed that the smell of tallow is loathsome to her" (I, 5, 83-84). She objects to the smoky odor of her father's clothes and prefers not to walk with him in the street because of "a horror of appearing ridiculous even in the eyes of vulgar Trebians" (I, 6, 112). Her disgust at whatever is vulgar or socially low, be it an odor or a manner, points to a kind of inhibition—the socially low being equated with the instinctual. Anal concerns substitute for the forbidden, secret concerns, which in Esther are related to the secret of her father's (and her own infantile) past life.

Mr. Lyon, we are told, asked Esther as a child never to question him about her mother. The barrier of silence creates a blank in her life which seems to be the source of her inhibited development. She does not express resentment directly against the father who guards the secret. But she finds a substitute gratification for her curiosity through reading Byron and French novels—a substitute which also acts as a disguised outlet for resentment against the devout father whose heart's desire is to see her "fit to become a member of the church." Her sexual attraction to Felix merges with a wish to "learn the secret" of his moral ardor (which is, as we will see, a secret closely related to her father's). That wish reaches "a point of irritated anxiety" strong enough to overcome momentarily Esther's fear of vulgarity, and she calls at his house despite the fact that she can "think of no devices that were not so transparent as to be undignified" (I, 22, 321).

It is the father's secret, however, which is revealed to

Esther first. The story of Mr. Lyon's past is not retold at this point in the novel, but we must review it here in order to see how it relates to the formation of Esther's character and how its revelations can bring about her release from intense concern with odors and manners.

Late one night the young Rufus Lyon, well secured in a devoted ministerial career, and staunchly above any personal need for a wife, comes upon a beautiful young woman with babe-in-arms who beseeches him to save them from starvation. He rescues the woman and baby, Annette and Esther, and instantly falls passionately in love with the young mother—to the destruction of his career and the agony of his conscience. After a year of comforting and feeding them, he finally reveals his secret passion. When it is not warmly welcomed by Annette, Lyon falls dangerously ill and is fed and cared for by her. Once recovered, he marries her and three years later she dies (I, 6, 114-30).

Mr. Lyon, now known to be Esther's stepfather, regards his story as a confession of "weakness and error," but to Esther it is "a revelation of another sort: her mind seemed enlarged by a vision of passion and struggle, of delight and renunciation" (II, 26, 24). The immediate emphasis is on the "new sympathy" for her "odd, wayworn, unworldly" stepfather, a sympathy in which she "felt herself exalted." And the moral significance of the change is underlined:

Perhaps this knowledge would have been less powerful within her but for the mental preparation that had come during the last two months from her acquaintance with Felix Holt, which had taught her to doubt the infallibility of her own standard, and raised a presentiment of moral depths that were hidden from her. (II, 26, 25)

But Esther has not just learned a moral lesson—she

has had the blank in her life replaced by a primal vision of "passion and struggle" which opens the "floodgates" of her feelings in many ways. She shows an intense interest in the contrast between her mother's social status ("She was well born—she was a lady") and her stepfather's poverty, which makes her own participation in the life of poverty chosen by Felix seem possible. As she sits alone "dwelling on the memories and the few remaining relics of her parents," she is more "oppressed" than usual by "the lingering odors of the early dinner," but she doesn't try to escape from them (II, 27, 29). She leaves "her curls all pushed back carelessly" even when Felix comes, and walks out with him not caring, as she always had, about appearances.

Her release, at this point, from disgust and fear of vulgarity (and its meaning as the instinctual) is understandable as a consequence of sexual enlightenment. At the same time she suddenly becomes more aware of her feeling for Felix. She yearns "for some expression of love" from him, and suffers from the sense that he "willed her exclusion from his life":

In her pain that his choice lay aloof from her, she was compelled frankly to admit to herself the longing that it had been otherwise, and that he had entreated her to share his difficult life. He was like no one else to her; he had seemed to bring at once a law, and the love that gave strength to obey the law. Yet the next moment, stung by his independence of her, she denied that she loved him; she had only longed for a moral support under the negations of her life. (II, 27, 43-44)⁶

She tries not to reveal too much to Felix, but she does tell him that she can imagine herself "choosing hardships as the better lot" in life.

---

⁶ At this point Esther seems to have arrived at Romola's starting point—with Felix portrayed as capable of fulfilling the idealized role that the father figures in *Romola* fell short of.

This avowal takes us back to the moral impact on Esther of hearing her father's story. If Felix Holt has given her a "presentiment of moral depths" that is enlarged by her father's story, we should be able to find moral depths in that story which will help to define the direction of her moral growth. But the moral of Lyon's story is confusing (which may be one reason for telling it hundreds of pages before it is supposed to have its effect on Esther). Thus, before I can go any further with my analysis of Esther's development, I will first have to turn to the history and character of Rufus Lyon.

II

On the manifest level the story of Rufus Lyon's romance may be intended as a confirmation of Felix Holt's theory that love of women is "a curse" which makes men abandon great purposes and become "slaves to the petty desires of petty creatures" (I, 10, 180). Before meeting Esther's mother, Mr. Lyon was a man of great purpose, a minister whose "passion" was "for doctrines, for argumentative conquest on the side of right" (I, 6, 115). But his high calling is undermined when he falls in love with Esther's mother. He can no longer totally devote himself to his religious faith, and, "achingly conscious of having fallen in a struggle," can only pray "that some great discipline might come . . . and the supreme facts become again supreme in his soul" (I, 6, 124-25).[7] Thus the moral message would be: don't let this happen to you—because "to the end of men's struggles a penalty will remain for those who sink from the ranks of the

[7] Compare this expression of guilt and longing for discipline with similar crises in Maggie Tulliver and Godfrey Cass.

heroes"; or, don't be one of the women who bring about such disasters. As such, the second half of the moral could be applied to Esther, indicating that her idealism develops from an inspired resolution not to be such a "curse."

This interpretation would account for some of the later attempts to give Esther's choice of "the ordinary lot of womanhood" superego status as part of a new idealism which requires difficult renunciation. But the account of Mr. Lyon's romance cannot support such an interpretation. Annette is not a Rosamond Vincy, or "petty creature" whose desires enslave anyone. Even Mr. Lyon himself, who never ceases to view his love as a sinful lapse from a higher purpose, puts the blame on his own nature. George Eliot is surely aware of the disparity between Felix Holt's theory and Rufus Lyon's experience. But her attitude toward the kind of idealism in which there is no room for sexuality is apparently confused enough to allow for such disparity.

What I see in the fall of Rufus Lyon (and have trouble believing that George Eliot did not see) is the temporary collapse of a deadening defense. The passion for doctrines, which is suddenly overcome by the sexuality it attempts to deny, is not simply one of our "pitiably narrow theories" which is "not quite large enough for all the disclosures of time" as the narrator apologetically implies (I, 6, 125). It is a defense with which George Eliot is intimately involved in *Romola*, and which she is almost ready to cast in the form of the sterile Casaubon in *Middlemarch*. But here she apparently still needs to idealize it in order to disguise the Oedipal and oral wishes that are fulfilled when it breaks down.

The love story itself is both Oedipal and oral. Lyon is

aware that his wish to marry the young mother he has rescued means displacing Esther's father, who is lost but may still be alive. He can't help being glad that Annette has lost the address where further inquiries about her husband could be made, and her disinclination to make contact with her relatives provides him with an excuse for making no inquiries through them. Since she is obviously too helpless to support herself, he "seemed" to have a reason for keeping her "under his own eyes" (I, 6, 123).

Like Tessa, Annette is "apparently so helpless, except as to the task of attending to her baby," that she is surrounded by oral imagery. She is "one of those angelic-faced helpless women who take all things as manna from Heaven," and "seemed to entertain as little concern about the strange world in which she lived as a bird in its nest: an avalanche had fallen over the past, but she sat warm and un-crushed—there was food for many morrows, and her baby flourished" (I, 6, 124). Thus Lyon's Oedipal love is combined with (and only somewhat disguised from himself as) the regressive longing for a mother's love: "he wished that he might call her his own, that he might worship her beauty, that *she* might love and caress *him*" (I, 6, 118; my emphasis). At first he must feed and comfort the orphans, but when he falls ill Annette feeds him and nurses him back to health.

All the while, Rufus Lyon is being tortured by his conscience which is both as tyrannical and as corruptible as Maggie's. It maintains a rigid either-or position, so that as long as there is "something he preferred to complete obedience" to his duty, he is subjected to its attacks and is miserable. Thus his romance, which contains elements of both the rescue fantasies in *Silas Marner*, ends in negation rather than rebirth. Instead of accepting Esther as the kind of treasure that Eppie is to Silas, Lyon feels that he has lost his treasure:

In these days his religious faith was not slumbering; it was awake and achingly conscious of having fallen in a struggle. He had had a great treasure committed to him, and had flung it away: he held himself a backslider. (I, 6, 124)

He reclaims his treasure, his high calling, after Annette's death; Esther is merely "the one visible sign of that four years' break in his life" (I, 6, 125). His conscience also cuts him off from the kind of rescue experienced by Godfrey Cass:

His love was the first love of a fresh young heart full of wonder and worship. But what to one man is the virtue which he has sunk below the possibility of aspiring to, is to another the backsliding by which he forfeits his spiritual crown. (I, 6, 122)

At one point it seems as if oral gratification in the form of mothering might be approved by Lyon's superego. The "slow and gentle death" of Annette is for him "a period of such self-suppression and life in another as few men know." His three years of caring for her mean untiring work and patience and more "thorough renunciation than he had ever known in the time of his complete devotion to his ministerial career" (I, 6, 129). But with Annette's death, Lyon returns to his career and leaves mothering behind by sending Esther away to be "so educated as to be able to get her own bread in case of his death."

The latent content of Lyon's romance, despite the confusing moral attached to it, provides important clues to the shifting allegiances and pressures in George Eliot's mind. The oral-Oedipal-rescue fantasy reassembles wishes that have been fragmented and scattered since the destructive flood in *The Mill on the Floss.*[8] The fantasy is anxiously warded off by the Rufus Lyon in her mind, but not so stringently by the more flexible Esther, for whom the primal scene is a release as well as a cause for a different kind of moralizing. The tremendous surge of love for her father, which is Esther's first response to his story, must mean that his "passion and struggle" have made him more fully human in her eyes. How else could his account, in which he fails to show much capacity for loving her, produce such a response? She tells Felix that the story "has made me see things I was blind to before—depths in my father's nature" (II, 23, 31). She does not—at least yet—say "moral depths." She also comes away with a new knowledge of her mother which is the beginning of another kind of growth.

The apparently moral "illumination" that Esther gleans from her father's story is still somewhat unaccountable. She seems to ignore his rejection of sexual passion and love, and respond only to the intensity of his feeling for her mother, so that his sinful lapse becomes her ideal:

"But that must be the best life, father," said Esther, suddenly rising, with a flush across her paleness, and standing with her head thrown a little backward, as if some illumination had given her a new decision. "That must be the best life."

"What life, my dear child?"

---

[8] Rage and rebellion (except in the form of a punishing superego) remain separate from the wishes assembled here, but appear in relation to Felix Holt's less distinct primal confrontation. Despite this separation the process is under way. Libidinal impulses are coming together and beginning to assert a more unified pressure against exaggerated superego claims. The process points toward *Middlemarch.*

"Why, that where one bears and does everything because of some great and strong feeling—so that this and that in one's circumstances don't signify."

"Yea, verily; but the feeling that should be thus supreme is devotedness to the Divine Will."

Esther did not speak; her father's words did not fit on to the impressions wrought in her by what he had told her. (II, 26, 26-27)

Esther's "illumination" is moral in the sense that her vision of the good life is humanized—it is no longer defined by elegant surroundings, but by feeling. Thus when Esther tells Felix that she can imagine herself "choosing hardships," she must mean that she would choose love, which would make hardships insignificant. Such a choice would not be moral in the same sense that Rufus Lyon's or Felix Holt's choices are moral.

It is possible to argue that George Eliot is aware of the deficiencies of Rufus Lyon as a moral example for Esther, and of the disparity between Felix Holt's and Lyon's experiences. But the awkward handling of these characters suggest that she is uncertain—not in control. In Esther she presents us with a possibility that was not present in *Romola,* where id in the form of Tito was all bad, and superego in the form of Romola was all good. But she does not seem to trust the "strong feeling" that Esther thinks would make even a life of hardships meaningful. So Esther must still be tested by actualizing her old daydreams of elegance, and then saved by means of a "terrible vision." On the other hand, in Rufus Lyon the author presents us with a paragon of selflessness whose negations are made obvious and then obscured by an alternation between caricature and sentimental idealization.

Both before and after the flashback, Lyon is portrayed as a somewhat comical, eccentric figure who nevertheless is repeatedly singled out for admiration by the narrator. We are meant to smile tenderly at the little minister who "snatched at the details of life as if they were darting past him—as if they were like the ribbons at his knees, which would never be tied all day if they were not tied on the instant" (I, 16, 258). But we are cautioned not to feel too superior by a narrator who "never smiled at Mr. Lyon's trustful energy without falling to penitence and veneration immediately after." There follows a soaring idealization of unworldliness which is conspicuously out of tune with the novel as a whole and can only be laid to the author's uneasiness:

> For what we call illusions are often, in truth, a wider vision of past and present realities—a willing movement of a man's soul with the larger sweep of the world's forces—a movement towards a more assured end than the chances of a single life. We see human heroism broken into units and say, this unit did little—might as well not have been. But in this way we might break up a great army into units: in this way we might break the sunlight into fragments, and think that this and the other might be cheaply parted with. Let us rather raise a monument to the soldiers whose brave hearts only kept the ranks unbroken, and met death—a monument to the faithful who were not famous, and who are precious as the continuity of the sunbeams is precious, though some of them fall unseen and on barrenness. (I, 16, 266)

Is Rufus Lyon a "unit" of "human heroism," one of "the faithful," "precious as the continuity of the sunbeams," an unknown soldier who lacks a monument? Obviously not, but apparently the author is uncomfortable enough with Mr. Lyon's retreat from feelings to a "love of abstractions" to attempt to obscure it in this way.

Her treatment of Felix Holt betrays a similar uneasiness. Felix's fears, as well as his defenses, resemble

Rufus Lyon's. There is one long analytical section in which Felix is clearly set up as a moral example, the epitome of high-minded selflessness, who has struggled against and overcome a natural tendency toward violent anger. We are intended to come away impressed not only with Felix's self-mastery but also with his self-knowledge:

The weak point to which Felix referred was his liability to be carried completely out of his own mastery by indignant anger. His strong health, his renunciation of selfish claims, his habitual preoccupation with large thoughts and with purposes independent of everyday casualties, secured him a fine and even temper, free from moodiness or irritability. He was full of long-suffering towards his unwise mother, who "pressed him daily with words and urged him, so that his soul was vexed"; he had chosen to fill his days in a way that required the utmost exertion of patience, that required those little rill-like out-flowings of goodness which in minds of great energy must be fed from deep sources of thought and passionate devotedness. (II, 30, 71-72).

The passage goes on to imply that Felix fears his potential for violence, and it is clear, though not explicitly stated, that "he had chosen to fill his days in a way that required the utmost exertion of patience" in order to ward off his rage:

In this way his energies served to make him gentle; and now, in this twenty-sixth year of his life, they had ceased to make him angry, except in the presence of something that roused his deep indignation. When once exasperated, the passionateness of his nature threw off the yoke of a long-trained consciousness in which thought and emotion had been more and more completely mingled, and concentrated itself in a rage as ungovernable as that of boyhood. He was thoroughly aware of the liability, and knew that in such circumstances he could not answer for himself. (II, 30, 72)

Felix's devotion to political reform parallels Lyon's devotion to his higher calling, and likewise leaves no room for sexuality. He, too, has a sinful lapse in his past which he thrusts in all earnestness upon the shocked minister in an interview that is as comical as the analysis above is serious. "Do you believe in conversion?" Felix asks Mr. Lyon. "Yea, verily," is the reply. "So do I," continues Felix, "I was converted by six weeks' de-bauchery."

Despite the comedy, the means of Felix's conversion leaves no doubt as to the fears behind his devotion.

If I had not seen that I was making a hog of myself very fast, and that pig-wash, even if I could have got plenty of it, was a poor sort of thing, I should never have looked life fairly in the face to see what was to be done with it. I laughed out loud at last to think of a poor devil like me, in a Scotch garret, with my stockings out at heel and a shilling or two to be dissipated upon, with a smell of raw haggis mounting from below, and old women breathing gin as they passed me on the stairs—wanting to turn my life into easy pleasure. (I, 5, 87-88)

Thus Felix's debauch, leaving him with an impression of sexuality as bestial and degrading, turns him into a reformer. And the fact that his reforming begins at home underlines the primal and Oedipal significance of his experience. He abandons his medical apprenticeship and the "old women" who wanted to turn his life into "easy pleasure" and returns home to a mother who is seen in somewhat similar terms. He stops the sale of the "medicines" which his father has left as a provision for his mother—concoctions which at best "might as well be bottled ditch-water" (or pig-wash)—and Mrs. Holt feels that he does it "only to abuse his mother" (I, 4, 80).

Felix's knowledge of sexuality, like Esther's ignorance, produces a kind of anal distortion which keeps his mind focused on the things he finds disgusting. He sees the world he wants to reform as "tainted with pollution" (I, 27, 179) and his intense discontent is manifestly treated as a sign of high moral consciousness to be contrasted with Esther's petty distaste for vulgarity. But the blame that falls on "the foolish women who spoil men's lives" suggests that Felix's disgust originates in the unwelcome discovery of the mother's sexuality.[9] The hostility which predominates in his attitude toward women is accompanied by the idea of "one beautiful woman" with a mind as noble as her face is beautiful (II, 27, 38). As a phrenologist once told Felix, his head indicates a "large Ideality, which prevents him from finding anything perfect enough to be venerated" (I, 5, 95). Beauty is assumed to disguise a dangerous "curse" just as refinement of any kind is assumed to disguise "rottenness" (I, 5, 100). Thus Felix refuses to be one of "your ringed and scented men" and decides to rejoin the ranks of working men which his father made the mistake of leaving. He will never marry, but devote his life to purifying "the spawning life of vice and hunger" which sticks in his mind "like a splinter" (II, 27, 36).

There is one insightful comment on Felix which comes tantalizingly close to the interpretation I have just made. It comes from Mr. Lyon:

"The temptations that most beset those who have great natural gifts, and are wise after the flesh, are pride and scorn, more particularly towards those weak things of the world which have been chosen to confound the things which are mighty. The *scornful nostril and the high head gather not the odours that lie on the track of the truth.* The mind that is too ready at contempt and reprobation is . . . as a clenched fist that can give blows, but is

---

[9] See pp. 187-190 of my chapter on *Middlemarch*.

shut up from receiving and holding ought that is precious—
though it were heaven-sent manna." (I, 5, 94; my emphasis)

George Eliot is playing with Mr. Lyon's earnestness
here, just as she plays with the obvious exaggerations
in Felix's manner and appearance. Felix's habitual *for-
tissimo*, his shaggy massiveness, and his fondness for
"banging and smashing" are meant to be funny. And
through the comedy comes a sense that both of these
superego-ridden characters are to a certain extent seen
with a critical eye. But the author can't let the criticism
go too far. Felix must be seen as "gentle," "long-
suffering," "even-tempered," and "free from moodiness
or irritability" in order to insure his moral sigificance.
The author's own defensiveness has relaxed in this
novel far enough to let her create what she then feels
called upon to retract.

In the case of Felix's denial of sexuality and rage,
however, the retraction goes beyond the blurring of
idealization. At the outset his attraction and repulsion
toward Esther are revealed in the comic spirit, and
there is no reason to think that George Eliot is unaware
that more than moral disapproval is involved in Felix's
thoughts of coming every day to scold Esther and to
"make her cry and cut her fine hair off" (I, 5, 103).[10] But
later, when Esther's "irritated anxiety to see Felix" has
driven her to call at his home, the author has to falsify
Felix in order to make his "exquisite goodness" the
predominant ingredient in his influence. His "perfect
calm" is contrasted to Esther's agitation, and the au-

[10] As Ian Milner points out, this is "one of the many scenes in
George Eliot when the 'sub-text,' and the implied nuances of the
action, say more than and may even contradict the text." See *The
Structure of Values in George Eliot* (Prague, 1968), p. 61.

thor herself seems, for the moment, to forget that Felix's struggle against the sexual attraction (however unconscious) would have produced something less than such ease and placidity.[11]

The author's difficulty increases when she deals with Felix as a non-violent political reformer. On election day he tries to stay at home and hope for the best because he dreads "the prophetic wisdom that ends in desiring the fulfillment of its own evil forebodings" (II, 32, 102). When he finally rushes out in response to loud noises which "wrought more and more strongly on his imagination," he finds that order is already being restored. Esther's "probable alarm at the noises" makes him give way to "new reasons" for visiting her. He has come so far in his feeling for Esther that he needs to make a declaration—not of love, but of rejection. And he cannot resist the urge to let Esther know that it is not easy for him to reject her. The thoughts attributed to him afterward constitute another attempt to idealize his self-denial, but the defensiveness is nevertheless discernible:

Felix reproached himself. He would have done better not to speak in that way. But the prompting to which he had chiefly listened had been the desire to prove to Esther that he set a high value on her feelings. He could not help seeing that he was very important to her; and he was too simple and sincere a man to ape a sort of humility which would not have made him any the better if he had possessed it. Such pretences turn our lives into sorry dramas. And Felix wished Esther to know

11 Laurence Lerner, *The Truthtellers* (New York, 1967), pp. 49-50. The sentimentalized picture of Felix in this scene is nicely analyzed by Lerner, although I would have to take the causation he traces a step further. Felix is sentimentalized to suit George Eliot's moral purpose, but that moral purpose is, *a priori*, a defensive stance toward sexuality.

that her love was dear to him as the beloved dead are dear. He felt that they must not marry—that they would ruin each other's lives. But he had longed for her to know fully that his will to be always apart from her was renunciation, not an easy preference. In this he was thoroughly generous . . . (II, 32, 108-109)

She is as "dear to him as the beloved dead"? The defensiveness of Felix's renunciation betrays itself by having to "prove" (and declare by negation) the love that is being rejected.[12] And the supposed altruism in wanting Esther to know that her feelings matter is just another means of avoiding his own feelings and punishing her. Thus Felix goes on to feel "for Esther's pain as the strong soldier, who can march on hungering without fear that he shall faint, feels for the young brother—the maiden-cheecked conscript whose load is too heavy for him" (II, 32, 109).[13] But in spite of the author's attempt to make Felix "thoroughly generous" and noble in all this, the denied feelings are coming dangerously close to the surface and are about to erupt in another form.

Felix goes for a walk after leaving Esther, then turns back into town thinking "it would be better for him to look at the busy doings of men than to listen in solitude to the voices within him; and he wished to know how things were going on" (II, 33, 109). The last motive has the ring of a superfluous rationalization meant to disguise his attraction to the violence he abhors. He turns

[12] I am reminded of Will Ladislaw who feels he must renounce his love for Dorothea once her father-figure husband is dead. Esther's father is away on a journey when Felix is moved to declare his renunciation. In both cases the defense operates very efficiently to bring about disguised gratification.

[13] This transformation of Esther's sex is another sign of Felix's fear, or, better, the fear in the author of any dependent "hungering" relationship to a woman (i.e., a mother).

away from what is "within him" to find violence and chaos in which he takes part in spite of himself. Thus when we hear of the "mass of wild chaotic desires and impulses around him" we cannot help but relate them to the sexuality he has just renounced. (II, 33, 117).

During the course of the riot, Felix exchanges the big stick he always carries, first for a cudgel, then for a sword, and finally he is shot in the shoulder of "the arm that held the naked weapon" (II, 33, 123). The scene is repetitious and laden with variations of the "mass of wild chaotic desires"—all outside Felix—"shouts and roaring" (111), "pulling and scuffling," "deafening shouts," "blind outrages of the mad crowd"(114). Felix sees that the actions of the excited crowd "could hardly be counted on more than those of oxen and pigs congregated amidst hootings and pushings" (110). He thinks he has the power to influence these men "whose mental state was a mere medley of appetites and confused impressions" (118). He knows he is "incurring great risks; but 'his blood was up' " (119), and at this point, after seizing the constable's weapon in order to save him from the mob, Felix unintentionally kills him.

The total effect is that of another primal scene. The portrayal of the election-day riot reflects impressions left on the author's mind by an election riot witnessed in her youth. It has political implications for her as evidence of the "savage beast" that political institutions must control. But her portrayal of this riot reveals more than a political fear. The author tries to separate the rage in the crowd from Felix, whose concern is to control or divert its destructiveness. But even though Felix is said to have killed the constable unintentionally, rather than in an outburst of the uncontrollable rage he is capable of, the destructive fantasy emerges. The phallic weapons and the death of an authority-figure are Oedipal elements which, like the earlier scene of Oedipal intimidation, define Felix's tendency toward rage as an anal-sadistic regression from Oedipal conflict. But the regressive solution fails when Felix kills the constable and overestimates his power to "carry the dangerous mass out of mischief" (II, 33, 117).

At this point the author disposes of the titular hero by sending him to jail. For the rest of the novel he functions only as an ideal in Esther's mind. His removal is a more drastic retraction than his idealization, and suggests that the "dangerous mass" which prevails over Felix has revived in George Eliot the fear associated with the "dangerous masses" that capsized Tom and Maggie in *The Mill on the Floss*. If so, the author does not capitulate altogether. She explores the feared impulse of rage further, but in the character of Harold Transome, who is an anti-hero and not to be identified easily with his creator.

On the manifest level Harold Transome is presented as a contrast to Felix Holt.[14] Although "nature and fortune seemed to have done what they could to keep the lots of the two men quite aloof from each other" (I, 3, 71), they make a "considerable difference" in one another's lives. Both men call themselves radicals in politics—but their views are as dissimilar as their social circumstances. Both are "only sons" who are rebelling against their mothers in different ways. And they share a distinct disregard for women which seems to originate in the mother-son relationship.

In regard to fathers the comparison becomes more

14 See Kettle, *"Felix Holt, the Radical,"* pp. 101-3.

interesting. Felix, whose father is dead, rebels against him by abolishing his business. His antagonism to existing authority, as a substitute for the father, is an extension of that rebellion. And the man he kills is a father-figure in his function as a law officer and in his possession of the weapon Felix seizes. Harold *seems* to have a different attitude. He shows more genuine concern for the debilitated Mr. Transome, wrongly supposed to be his father, than he does for his mother. And he is given enough external reasons for hating Jermyn, who turns out to be his actual father, to veil somewhat the Oedipal nature of that rebellion. But his reasons for hating Jermyn, even before the crucial disclosure, have a discernibly Oedipal cast: he sees Jermyn as the exploiter of his mother, and is particularly enraged when she seems to protect such a man. Thus the apparent contrast between Felix and Harold is at one level a parallel. The crucial confrontation between Harold and Jermyn takes place during a meeting concerning Felix Holt's fate and gathers some of the intensity and significance of his rebellion.

Harold Transome is presented as a sensual egotist— but not one as extreme as Tito. The limits of his egotism are defined by comparison with Jermyn. Harold is a "determined lizard" (I, 1, 31) whose practical effectiveness depends upon a narrow imagination. But his nature is "less animally forcible, less unwavering in selfishness" than Jermyn's (II, 35, 131). The conflict of interests between the father and son threatens Jermyn with financial ruin—a doom which brings out his "latent savageness" (I, 2, 55), the "impulses . . . of a hunted brute" who has no "scruples" (II, 47, 311). And Jermyn's revelations about the entail on the Transome estate threaten Harold more subtly: he sees that his "weapon" against Jermyn may be "wrenched out of his hands" (II, 47, 311).

What I see in the confrontation which brings both men to the point of murderous violence is not only Harold being forced to see Jermyn as his father, or his father's nature in himself, but George Eliot facing the rage and the savage beast that she fears. The violence in Jermyn is not surprising, but the same impulse in Harold is as much a revelation as the hated fatherhood:

He started and looked round into Jermyn's eyes. For an instant, which seemed long, there was no sound between them, but only angry hatred gathering in the two faces. Harold felt himself going to crush this insolence: Jermyn felt that he had words within him that were fangs to clutch this obstinate strength, and wring forth the blood and compel submission. (II, 47, 313).

Harold strikes Jermyn across the face with his whip on the instant that his mother is mentioned. Jermyn responds by clutching Harold "hard by the clothes just below the throat, pushing him slightly so as to make him stagger." When Harold threatens to be the death of him, Jermyn uses his ultimate weapon: "Do, said Jermyn, in a grating voice; *I am your father.*"

In the thrust by which Harold had been made to stagger backward a little, the two men had got very near the long mirror. They were both white; both had anger and hatred in their faces; the hands of both men were upraised. As Harold heard the last terrible words he started at a leaping throb that went through him, and in the start turned his eyes away from Jermyn's face. He turned them on the same face in the glass with his own beside it, and saw the hated fatherhood reasserted. (II, 47, 314)

The effect of this scene on Harold is simply treated: "All the pride of his nature rebelled against his sonship" (II,

48, 37). He tries to prove that he has no "inherited meanness" by doing what "perfect honor" demands in regard to Esther (II, 48, 320). The "iron" has "entered his soul" for the first time, and self-knowledge (though it is not stressed as such) leads to a determination to be better.

For the author, the scene has greater implications. We have seen brute violence in other fathers: in Mr. Tulliver's beating of Wakem, and Baldassare's strangling of Tito. But here the son is forced to see the brutality of the father in himself. In terms of George Eliot's reintegration, this is a significant step. It goes beyond Felix Holt's awareness that he is capable of violence when his moral indignation is aroused. In Harold Transome's case there is no moral indignation to excuse the violence. There is only the hated father. But, as we have seen, in order to create such a confrontation the author had to drop her hero and give a less sympathetic character the stage.

III

Harold's vision of himself beside Jermyn in the mirror is a prelude to the "terrible vision" that saves Esther. Mrs. Transome's lonely agony after Harold's rejection, drives her to seek compassion from Esther, who is pondering the choice she must make between wealth and poverty, Harold Transome and Felix Holt. Mrs. Transome's suffering "pierced Esther to the heart," and the "dreary waste of years empty of sweet trust and affection, afflicted her even to horror" (II, 50, 332-33). The experience "seemed to have come as a last vision to urge her towards the life where the draughts of joy sprang from the unchanging fountains of reverence and devout love."

On the manifest level Esther's "terrible vision" is meant to be a decisive factor in her moral growth and in her choice of Felix and hardship. The scene itself is intensely convincing. But the language used to describe the life toward which the vision moves Esther—the "draughts of joy" and the "unchanging fountains of reverence and devout love"—is disconcertingly vague, lofty, and unrelated to Esther's experience either in her own home or with Felix Holt or at Transome Court. And Esther's return to her father and Felix seems pale and unconvincing beside the embrace of the two women.

Perhaps the best appreciation of George Eliot's conscious intention regarding Esther's moral growth is given by Barbara Hardy. She cites the details showing that "Mrs. Transome and Esther are carefully drawn in parallel.":

To begin with, there are carefully underlined resemblances in their presentation. Mrs. Transome has 'a high-born imperious air' and Esther "had too many airs and graces, and held her head much too high." Mr. Transome "shrank like a timid animal" when his wife appeared and Mr. Lyon found himself "in timorous subjection" to Esther's wishes. Both women are fastidious, accomplished, clever. Mrs. Transome "had secretly picked out for private reading the lighter parts of dangerous French authors—and in company had been able to talk of Mr. Burke's style, or of Chateaubriand's eloquence—had laughed at the Lyrical Ballads and admired Mr. Southey's Thalaba." Esther makes her first appearance to defend Byron: " 'I have a great admiration for Byron'" she says, when Felix has knocked the book down and picked it up to abuse it. Felix's denunciation of the Byronic heroes as "the most paltry puppets that were ever pulled by the strings of lust and pride" echoes Mrs. Transome's reading list, "She was interested in stories of illicit passion." The insistent details make a kind of fluidity in the novel—the relationship of the characters challenges us to see them temporarily as doubles.[15]

Mrs. Hardy goes on to suggest that this doubling exists for "a decided moral emphasis: Esther escapes the temptation of her romantic dreams of love and this decomposition of character underlines the narrowness of her escape." She adds, justly, that there is a "kind of human optimism rising above any one individual failure" in the juxtaposition of the tragedy of one with the redemption of the next.

This is a fine analysis, but does not account for the necessity of the final vision. If we are discontent with the moral stress given to the scene between Esther and Mrs. Transome, it may be because Esther's moral preference is clearly established long before that scene.[16] If there was any doubt about it after her "illumination" before coming to Transome Court, the doubt is certainly dispelled in the courtroom scene where "her woman's passion and her reverence for rarest goodness rushed together in an undivided current" (II, 46, 301). Her preference for Felix over Harold is also established before this. She enjoys her sense of "power" over Harold, as well as his "homage," but "there was a vague consciousness that the love of this not unfascinating man who hovered about her gave an air of moral mediocrity to all her prospects" (II, 43, 241). He is fascinating, perhaps, but she does not love him. To homage and power she distinctly prefers the sense of "dependence

[15] *The Novels of George Eliot* (London, 1959), 137-38.

[16] Hardy, pp. 62-63, argues that Esther's development is "treated with tragic gravity," and that her "moral choice does not carry the conviction of a tragic ordeal" because she has "too much to gain" by it. But I suggest that the kind of intensity she refers to as "tragic" has a source deeper than the manifest moral choice.

and possible illumination" that she has with Felix. She may even prefer the "sense of inferiority and just subjection" (II, 43, 239). The only problem that remains at the time of her "terrible vision" is that "the presence and the love of Felix Holt—was only a quivering hope, not a certainty" (II, 49, 326).

This uncertainty is not changed by Esther's "terrible vision." And since Esther was ready to pay the "heavy price" for Felix long before this if only he would ask it, we are left to account for the scene in other than moral terms. It is the emotional climax of the novel, and it is extremely necessary as a culmination of the latent "family romance" pattern which began with Mr. Lyon's disclosure of Esther's highborn parentage.[17] Esther's daydream-come-true at Transome Court is, like the typical family romance, an apparent rejection of parents that aims at reconciliation. The reconciliation with the rejected lowly father is achieved easily, as an immediate response to his story. But Esther's reconciliation with a mother in Mrs. Transome is more difficult.

The suggestions of a mother-daughter relationship between Esther and Mrs. Transome are aspects of doubling not included in Mrs. Hardy's analysis. Before Esther goes to live at Transome Court her memories of her lost mother have been emphasized. Her need for a mother and her gradually developing sympathies find a perfect outlet in Mrs. Transome's need for comfort and understanding. Twice Mrs. Transome expresses the wish that Esther were her daughter in response to the "delicate care" that is taken to please her. And for Esther "there was a peculiar interest in Mrs. Transome," for an "elderly woman" was a "new figure" in

[17] See Freud, "Family Romance," *Standard Edition,* IX, 237.

her experience. She sees her behavior toward Mrs. Transome as coming from a "daughter's feeling" which "any young woman" has "towards an older one who has been kind to her" (II, 45, 278). She even looks like Mrs. Transome's daughter, as Denner remarks: "'. . . what a hand and instep she has, and how her head is set on her shoulders—almost like your own, Madam'" (II, 39, 195).

The mother-daughter undercurrent culminates in the scene which gives Esther her "terrible vision." When Mrs. Transome sees the light from Esther's window, she thinks:

> There was mercy in her young heart; she might be a daughter who had no impulse to punish and to strike her whom fate had stricken. On the dim loneliness before her she seemed to see Esther's gentle look; it was possible still that the misery of this night might be broken by some comfort. The proud woman yearned for the caressing pity that must dwell in that young bosom. She opened her door gently, but when she had reached Esther's she hesitated. She had never in her life asked for compassion—had never thrown herself in faith on an unproffered love.(II, 50, 332)

Mrs. Transome does not knock; Esther hears her, opens the door and leads her in by the hand. The signs of Mrs. Transome's suffering "pierced Esther to the heart."

> A passionate desire to soothe this suffering woman came over her. She clung round her again, and kissed her poor quivering lips and eyelids, and laid her young cheek against the pale and haggard one. Words could not be quick or strong enough to utter her yearning. As Mrs. Transome felt that soft clinging, she said,—
> "God has some pity on me." (II, 50, 332-33)

After her moral vision Esther tells Mrs. Transome that she will "seem to have a mother again" if she can take care of her. The older woman "yielded at last, and let Esther soothe her with a daughter's tendance" (II,

50, 334). Thus the reconciling process of the family romance is completed. The transgressing and unloving mother (like the father) is humanized, forgiven, and loved again.

F. R. Leavis dismisses Esther as "interesting only in relation to other feminine studies of the author's, and to her treatment in general of feminine charm."[18] As always there is an element of truth in what he says. Esther is not as interesting as her predecessors, nor does her development—which is the unifying force in the novel—succeed fully in holding its disparate elements together. The author's most intense impulses are expressed through other characters, while Esther is to some extent a neutral vehicle for approaching those extremes. Nevertheless I agree with Ian Milner that she is "an integral part of George Eliot's vision" and that her turning toward love cannot be dismissed as a "meliorist" touch intended to "relieve any unredeemed final tragedy."[19]

Only through Esther, I think, can we comprehend the whole state of mind represented in the novel. Without her we have a state of irresolvable polarity: the self-denying superego-driven characters (Felix Holt, Rufus Lyon) on one hand, and the self-seeking instinct-ridden characters (Mrs. Transome, Harold, Jermyn) on the other. The centrality of Esther reflects the integrating agency in the author's mind, and should not be ignored. George Eliot certainly has greater imaginative success with Mrs. Transome, whose isolated state of despair emerges from the author's experience. But the objec-

[18] *The Great Tradition* (New York, 1964), p. 52.

[19] Milner, *The Structure of Values,* pp. 64-65. Milner is referring to Miriam Allott's opinion in "George Eliot in the 1860's," *Victorian Studies* 5 (December 1961): 93-108.

tivity she maintains toward her character depends, as I see it, upon the parallel creation of Esther.

In one sense the intensity that comes through Mrs. Transome is a direct expression of feelings that most of George Eliot's creations struggle against: lovelessness, powerlessness, restrained rage, isolation, hate. In another sense it is through the creation of Mrs. Transome—a terrible mother in the ultimate sense of having hated and wished for the death of her own child—that these feelings finally connect with their source. When the "bad" mother has been made to endure all the painful emotions of the abandoned child, she is comforted and forgiven by the mother-deprived Esther.[20]

The mother-daughter reconciliation is indeed a turning point in Esther's development. It releases the energy needed to bind together the "heap of fragments" that has been her life (I, 15, 249). She has symbolically confronted the loneliness she fears, the loveless state that is worse than poverty, and having faced her ultimate fear she is released from her defenses against it.

George Eliot does not explore Esther's confrontation fully or freely. What I have described is partly its potential rather than its realized achievement. The analyses of previous novels leave us with little doubt about what is being avoided here. Behind all the oral dependency and hunger for love are the rage and resentment that, until now, seem to have prevented the creation of a "bad" mother. The creation of Mrs. Transome represents the return of a rigidly repressed memory, and a release of great significance for the author's self-discovery.

Esther's return to her father and to Felix takes her

[20] See my concluding chapter, pp. 221-223.

beyond Romola's mothering resolution. It is not, like her response to Felix in prison, "the movement of a frightened child toward its protector" (II, 45, 284). It is an acceptance of her dependency on a man who satisfies both her desires and her conscience. If the union of Esther and Felix is not fully realized as a distinct affirmation of libidinal as well as superego claims, it presents a possibility of more than the "faint rainbow on the blackness" offered in *Romola*.

Five

Middlemarch

Between *Felix Holt* and *Middlemarch* George Eliot returned to her poetic drama, *The Spanish Gypsy,* still determined to portray the rejection of marriage for a great public cause. This re-widening of the gap between desire and duty comes as no surprise now that the terms of the author's inner conflict are familiar. The surge of assertiveness on the side of duty seems to be an almost inevitable counter-move after the conception of Esther, through whom the author brings "woman's passion" and "reverence for rarest goodness" so close together that it is hard to determine which has the upper hand. Felix Holt's failure to ward off rage would have a similar tendency to intensify counter-instinctual demands.

Nevertheless, George Eliot's struggles with *Romola* and *Felix Holt* have produced some positive results. The dreariness of Romola's selfless end and the contrasting liveliness of Esther's love (reverence aside) show a discernible alteration in the author's attitude toward the opposing forces within—a change which improves the bargaining powers of id against superego. Thus in *The*

Spanish Gypsy the heroine's rejection of marriage, unlike
Maggie's in *The Mill on the Floss*, is seen as regrettable, a
loss of something basically good. Frederick Harrison,
who so admired *Felix Holt* that he reread it four or five
times, felt that Fedalma's grand submission was a "trea-
son to human life."[1] And in *Middlemarch* the author
herself seems to be approaching such an attitude.

The emotional impact that *Middlemarch* is apt to have
on a reader can best be described as a slightly melancholy sense of "unattained goodness."[2] Most of the
early reviews of the novel record such an impression,
which is one that I share.[3] The author seems to be at
once disillusioned and resigned. There is no feeling of
elation at the emergence of the instinctual self—
although that is the process I am about to describe in
Dorothea. George Eliot still has an emotional invest-
ment in the strict ideal of self-denial which seems, in
Middlemarch, to be seen as a glorious illusion.

Despite the undercurrent of regret, however, the
novel imparts a sense of completion and reconciliation
which reflects the author's total state of mind. Most of
the characters in *Middlemarch* find their aspirations,
however great or small, unfulfilled. But the kind of
vision that is able to enter into all of these characters is in
itself a fulfillment. The "various elements of the story,"
according to the author's own account, had been
"soliciting [her] mind for years—asking for a complete
embodiment."[4] The elements are not new—we have

[1] Haight, p. 405.

[2] See the Prelude to *Middlemarch* where the author's description of
Saint Theresa leads into chap. 1, "Miss Brooke."

[3] See John Holmstrom and Laurence Lerner, eds., *George Eliot and
Her Readers* (New York, 1966), pp. 117-18.

[4] Haight, p. 420.

seen all of them in earlier novels. But the way they are looked at is new. Their "complete embodiment" awaited the relaxation (if not cessation) of hostilities within the author, so that the conflict between duty and desire, superego and id, could become the subject matter rather than the driving and blinding force behind her fiction.

Thus the new kind of vision I am postulating here does not imply a sudden or drastic change in the author. It is another stage in the process of painful readjustment which has been traced through the novels succeeding *The Mill on the Floss*. As might be expected there are events in George Eliot's outer life which help to account for the diminution of superego demands apparent at this stage. By the end of 1868 George Eliot had achieved not only fame and financial independence, but also a kind of social acceptance. The Priory had become "the centre of the most interesting society in London," and many of the visitors by this time were women.[5] The author's journal records the effect of this change: "We have made some new friendships that cheer us with the sense of new admiration of acutal living beings whom we know in the flesh, and who are kindly disposed to us. And we have no real trouble."[6]

When trouble did come, with the agonizing illness and death of Lewes's son Thornton, it "cut deeper" than George Eliot expected. She had already begun *Middlemarch* with the background of Lydgate and the early Vincy and Featherstone scenes. But nursing and entertaining Thorny took precedence over her work. Before he died she began writing "The Legend of Jubal," a poem in which death brings "new awareness of the

[5] Ibid., p. 406. Earlier, respectable women did not call on the scandalous Mrs. Lewes.

[6] Ibid., p. 413.

value of life." And this new awareness stayed with her. Thornie's death brought George Eliot into "a permanently closer companionship with death" so that even after a long, quiet retreat in the country, she still felt "a deep sense of change within."[7]

After a year filled with travel aimed at restoring Lewes to health, the author began a story about Miss Brooke. She soon decided to take up *Middlemarch* again, combining the new story with those already begun, (the Lydgate, Vincy, and Featherstone scenes). The summer of 1870 was spent at Shottermill, where George Eliot's new awareness of the value of life was sustained by vistas that gave her a "sense of standing on a round world." She "wrote with less torment from diffidence and self-mistrust than she had felt in many years."[8]

Middlemarch is a novel without a hero or heroine. The author's state of mind is most directly embodied in a narrator who enters with equal perspicacity and nearly equal sympathy into the inner struggles of all the characters. Through him, the author consistently guides the reader toward the reevaluation of his first and even second impressions and judgments, and thus toward a continuing process of comparison and readjustment. The narrator's effectiveness in this role has been thoroughly appreciated and demonstrated by U. C. Knoepflmacher, who contrasts the helplessness of the observer of Maggie's tragic end to the kind of control we see in *Middlemarch:*

The narrator modulates our responses through accumulation. His effects are additive, incremental. As we progress in the narrative and move from one plot to the other, we constantly

[7] Ibid., p. 422, quoting *Letters,* V, 70.
[8] Ibid., pp. 432-33.

must take new stock of all that has gone before. Words like "opinion," "ardor," "Providence" gain new shades of meaning, while retaining their former connotations; metaphors appear in new contexts, creating unexpected links to their earlier usage.[9]

The result of this process is a widening of the reader's understanding and sympathy.

The narrator's activity, in other words, resembles the function of the ego that is able to balance and mediate between the conflicting claims of id and superego. His guidance gratifies a desire for integration and balance which the author encourages the reader to share. In previous novels we have been encouraged to see the contrast between egoist and altruist, between desire and duty, and to share the protagonist's choice of the "higher" motivation. But in *Middlemarch* the narrator shows us one mixed with the other and both as obstacles to the kind of openness and breadth of vision that would allow integration within the characters and effective communication between them.

Because of the constant readjustment of vision that characterizes *Middlemarch*, analyzing it is a delicate undertaking. My focus in the following analysis will thus be circumscribed enough to permit a careful exploration of only one aspect of the novel. The narrator, I think, has been thoroughly treated by U. C. Knoepflmacher and W. J. Harvey,[10] and I have only attempted to relate his function to my own approach to the novels. But the relationship between the author and the central characters has produced a certain amount of dissension among critics and can profit from further elaboration in

[9] *Laughter and Despair* (Berkeley and Los Angeles, 1971), p. 188.
[10] In addition to Knoeplfmacher's *Laughter and Despair* see Harvey's *The Art of George Eliot* (London, 1961), chap. 3.

psychoanalytic terms. The basic aim of my analysis will be to show how the author's inner equilibrium is reflected in the presentation of her major characters. I find that the characters in *Middlemarch* are much more fully developed than their predecessors, that the conscious presentation of their preoccupations most often converges rather than conflicts with the latent fantasies, and that the author's greater freedom in exploring both egoistic and altruistic motives leads her to new insights which replace some of the evasions and distortions of earlier novels.

Because Dorothea's development is a crucial issue in establishing that George Eliot's decade of struggle finally results in new knowledge and acceptance of herself, Part I of my analysis will explore the author's control of Dorothea and her emergence from the inner conflict leading to Maggie's death in *The Mill on the Floss*. The character of Casaubon, as a reflection of the neurotic needs underlying Dorothea's altruistic longings, will belong to this discussion. Part II concentrates on the character of Will Ladislaw and his significance as Dorothea's choice of husband. It will include the Fred Vincy-Mary Garth relationship, which somewhat parallels that of Dorothea and Will. Part III will focus on Lydgate, whose development closely parallels that of Dorothea and constitutes the reevaluation of a similar ideal. Rosamond and Bulstrode enter here, primarily for the light they shed on the unconscious needs expressed through Lydgate.

I

According to F. R. Leavis, *Middlemarch* is the only work of George Eliot which "can, as a whole (though not without qualification), be said to represent her mature genius."[11] He admires the "great intellectual powers" demonstrated in George Eliot's investigation of society and of individuals. The need for qualification lies in the conception of Dorothea, who is, according to Leavis, "a product of George Eliot's own 'soul-hunger'—another day-dream ideal self."[12] He carefully points out his approval of the opening chapters in which Dorothea "is not exempted from the irony that informs her vision of the other characters," so that at first "it looks as if George Eliot had succeeded in bringing within her achieved maturity this most resistant and incorrigible self."[13] But as early as the third chapter Leavis finds indications that the heroine is being exempted from irony, and he argues that ultimately we are meant to see Dorothea exactly as Will Ladislaw sees her, and as the "Prelude" prepares us to see her:

Dorothea, with her 'genius for feeling nobly', that 'current' in her mind 'into which all thought and feeling were apt sooner or later to flow—the reaching forward of the whole consciousness towards the fullest truth, the least partial good' (end of Chapter XX), and with her ability to turn that current into a passion for Will Ladislaw, gives us Maggie's case again, and Maggie's significance: again we have the confusions represented by the exalted vagueness of Maggie's 'soul-hunger'; we have the unacceptable valuations and the day-dream self-indulgence.[14]

Doubtless at certain moments George Eliot's understanding of Dorothea is temporarily eclipsed by identification. But "unacceptable valuations" do not

---

[11] *The Great Tradtion* (New York, 1964), p. 61.
[12] Ibid., p. 75.
[13] Ibid., pp. 73-74.
[14] Ibid., pp. 77.

predominate. Numerous critics have suggested that Leavis ignores some important criticism and ironies aimed at Dorothea, that his judgment underestimates the complexity and flexibility of the narrative voice in *Middlemarch,* and the constant alteration demanded of the reader's sympathy.[15] Knoepflmacher, for example, describes the narrator's attempts to check "our overeagerness to identify with Dorothea's ardent heart" in her dramatic scene with Lydgate, by interrupting Lydgate's adoration with a reminder that Dorothea's "shortsighted knowledge" of "lower experience" was "little helped by her imagination."[16]

There is an abundance of such evidence of George Eliot's control which Leavis's eloquent charge overlooks. Nevertheless, a certain amount of confusion remains both about the degree of her success, and about what kind of person Dorothea is and how the reader is meant to feel about her ultimate fate. Does she change in the course of the novel? If so, how does she change? And just how much does she change? Leavis's criticism assumes that, at least from the time of her disillusionment with Casaubon, Doroteha is a static character. Ian Milner, on the other hand, argues that Dorothea is "not merely the victim of moral idealism"

[15] See Derek Oldfield, "The Language of the Novel," in *"Middlemarch": Critical Approaches to the Novel,* ed. Barbara Hardy (New York, 1967), p. 69, passim; Mark Schorer, "The Structure of the Novel," ibid., pp. 23-24; Barbara Hardy, *The Novels of George Eliot* (London, 1959), pp. 155-84; R. T. Jones, *George Eliot* (Cambridge, 1970), pp. 62-63, passim; Ian Milner, *The Structure of Values in George Eliot* (Prague, 1968), pp. 72-73; Harvey, *The Art of George Eliot,* pp. 191-93; and Knoepflmacher, *Laughter and Despair,* pp. 170, 175, 178-79. Also Isobel Armstrong, *"Middlemarch: A Note on George Eliot's 'Wisdom,' "* in *Critical Essays on George Eliot,* ed. Barbara Hardy (New York, 1970), pp. 26-130 passim.

[16] *Laughter and Despair,* p. 172.

but a character whose inner conflict results in "coming to terms with her own nature and its needs."[17] Nevertheless he is uncertain about the relationship of Will Ladislaw to Dorothea's development. He cannot connect the emerging sensuality which he sees in Dorothea with the "quasi-reverential bodiless ecstasy" which is substituted for the portrayal of "the experience of passionate love" between Dorothea and Will Ladislaw.[18]

A psychoanalytic interpretation of Dorothea's role in the latent content of *Middlemarch* not only brings out more evidence of Dorothea's inner conflict and growth, it reveals an intimate relationship between that conflict and her moral idealism, and accounts for the quality of her relationship with Will Ladislaw. It reveals Dorothea as a character whose sensual nature is not suddenly freed from repression either through her disillusionment with Casaubon or at his death, but emerges painfully and reluctantly from one ruined ideal only to be subjected to the distortions of another ideal and another disillusionment before it finally comes to light. The latent content reaffirms the similarities (noted by Leavis) between Dorothea's longings and Maggie's; but more important, it shows the *differences* in emotional maturity manifested in their final attitudes. Maggie's conflicts lead her to a wished-for death. Dorothea's culminate in affirmation and greater self-acceptance— not in "Maggie's case again."

If we begin by looking at Dorothea's behavior apart from the narrator's attitudes toward her, we can see that her idealism is an attempt to order and elevate her life. She is impatient with her uncle's incoherent talk

[17] *The Structure of Values*, pp. 71-72
[18] Ibid., pp. 71, 83.

and his "way of 'letting things be' on his estate";[19] she
insists on "regulating life" according to her notions,
which include making improvements, fasting, "sitting
up at night to read old theological books," and dressing
plainly, wihtout "trimmings" or concern for fashion.
Dorothea is "bewitching" on horseback, enjoys riding
"in a pagan sensuous way," and looks forward "to renouncing it." She is both sensitive and incongruous on
the subject of self-mortification: she cannot bear to
hear her giving-up characterized as self-indulgence,
what she "likes" to do, or to be interpreted as immod-
estly attributing to herself grand motives; and she is, as
Celia says, inconsistent, for she allows herself the
"indulgence" of horseback riding in spite of "conscien-
tious qualms," just as she decides to keep her mother's
emeralds in spite of her rejection of ornaments. Celia is
kept in awe of Dorothea's attitude of "Puritanic toleration," and of the "scorching quality" of her speech and
quick anger. Dorothea speaks "with more energy than
is expected of so young a lady," and is irritated whenever her uncle makes a deprecating remark about the
intellectual capacities of young ladies. She definitely
presides in her uncle's household, and she likes both
authority and the homage it entails (chaps. 1, 2).

All of this behavior clearly demonstrates what the
narrator later refers to as the "coercion" which
Dorothea's religious disposition . . . exercised over her
life" (chap. 3). We are meant to see very clearly that
Dorothea's ardent nature is "hemmed in" in the first
place by internal strictures of her own choosing. After
this exposition we find the passage describing the ex-

[19] George Eliot, *Middlemarch,* ed. Gordon S. Haight, Riverside Edition
(Boston, 1956), chap. 1. Subsequent references are to this edition.

ternal conditions of education and society by which she is also "hemmed in," the passage which Leavis cites as the first indication of George Eliot's "unqualified self-identification" with Dorothea:

> For a long while she had been oppressed by the indefiniteness which hung in her mind, like a thick summer haze, over all her desire to make her life greatly effective. What could she do, what ought she to do? . . . The intensity of her religious disposition, the coercion it exercised over her life, was but one aspect of a nature altogether ardent, theoretic, and intellectually consequent: and with such a nature struggling in the bands of a narrow teaching, hemmed in by a social life which seemed nothing but a labyrinth of petty courses, a walled-in maze of small paths that led no whither, the outcome was sure to strike others as at once exaggeration and inconsistency.[20]

Leavis finds "something dangerous in the way the irony seems to be reserved for the provincial background and circumstances, leaving the heroine immune," but there are several reasons to question his conclusion. The passage does emphasize the external conditions, but it does so only after George Eliot has fully dramatized the internal dictates which restrict Dorothea's nature. Her scruples give her clear indications of what she should *not* do, but leave her feeling very hazy about what she *should* do.

The above passage closes with a statement, omitted by Leavis, hinting that Dorothea's passionate nature will not be contained by the mold she has chosen:

> The thing which seemed to her best, she wanted to justify by the completest knowledge; and not to live in a pretended admission of rules which were never acted on. Into this soul-hunger *as yet* all her youthful passion was poured; the union

[20] *The Great Tradition*, p. 74 (quoting from *Middlemarch*, chap. 3).

which attracted her was one that would deliver her from her girlish subjection to her own ignorance, and give her the freedom of voluntary submission to a guide who would take her along the grandest path (chap. 3; my emphasis).

"As yet" implies changes to come. The final sentence indicates that the immediate purpose of the passage is to make the reader understand Dorothea's choice of Casaubon. She wants to walk the "grandest path"—an ambitious aim which she alone can regard as a selfless ideal. Her desire to submit herself to a great teacher, like her other self-mortifying practices, is meant to be recognized as idealism well mixed with ambitious pride and illusion. We inevitably judge Dorothea by her choice of a husband, and are not expected to see it as an ideal act with which we uncritically identify ourselves, or with which George Eliot uncritically identifies herself. The author makes us aware that Dorothea's choice is made in accordance with an ideal image of herself rather than in accordance with her actual nature.

What the latent content adds to this picture is a succession of hints that behind Dorothea's subjection to an ideal image of herself there is a strong fear of sexuality which also influences her choice of a husband. Her "pagan sensuous" enjoyment of horseback riding and the urge to give it up, added to her attempt to "justify" sensual pleasure in emeralds ("It is strange how deeply colours seem to penetrate one, like scent") by "merging them in her mystic religious joy," demonstrate Dorothea's ambivalence toward sensuality. It is an ambivalence in which fear and rejection have the upper hand. Her blindness to Sir James's obvious attentions is part of this rejection. He is not conceivable as a possible suitor because he is seen in sensual terms: "dimpled hands" and "sleekly waving blonde hair" (chap. 3), and the complexion, in anger, of a *"cochon de lait"* (chap. 2). Thus when Celia suggests that Dorothea is "fond" of Sir James, she overreacts: "Fond of him, Celia! How can you choose such odious expressions?" (chap. 4). She has so patterned herself that her marriage will not be decided "by custom: good looks, vanity, and merely canine affection" (chap. 1), all sensual criteria.

These hints culminate in Dorothea's experience of Rome on her wedding journey when the fears underlying her rejection of sensuality emerge dramatically. First, however, George Eliot vividly portrays that rejection by placing Dorothea beside the reclining Ariadne for the purpose of the revealing antithesis.[21] Dorothea's form is not "shamed by" that of the statue. Her Quakerish drapery, however, imprisons Dorothea's "breathing life" as much as the cold marble imprisons the voluptuousness of the statue.[22] Dorothea's likeness to Ariadne also previews her forlorn feeling as she begins to discover that Casaubon will not be able to guide her out of the maze of her girlish ignorance. Dorothea is observed by Will Ladislaw and Naumann at this point,

---

[21] Jones, *George Eliot*, pp. 74–75; Hardy, "The Surface of the Novel," in *"Middlemarch": Critical Approaches to the Novel*, pp. 163–65.

[22] Chap. 19 is full of mythological references which corroborate this interpretation. Here the reclining Ariadne's sensuality is underlined by the author's remark that the statue was "then called the Cleopatra." The Theseus-Ariadne-Dionysus (Bacchus) references, here and in relation to Casaubon's labyrinthine work, relate back to *Romola* and reflect a distinct change in the author's attitude. Romola's marriage to Tito, commemorated in a painting of Bacchus and Ariadne, brings her to grief. But Dorothea's choice of Will Ladislaw (which parallels Ariadne's marriage to Dionysus after disappointment in Theseus) releases her from the labyrinth.

and Leavis objects that we are expected to see her as
Will sees her, not only as a beautiful form, but as "an
angel beguiled.[23] Actually in this scene we see Dorothea
as Naumann sees her, with his emphasis on her Quakerish drapery: he "would dress her as a nun" in his
picture (chap. 19). Will's view of Dorothea as "an
angel beguiled" (chap. 21) is soon qualified by his own
criticism, when he calls her rejection of art "the fanati-
cism of sympathy" (chap. 22). He suspects that she has
"some false belief in the virtues of misery," and remarks
that she talks as if she "had never known any youth," as
if she "had had a vision of Hades" in her childhood. Thus
his recognition of Dorothea as beguiled by her own
notions, and suffering from some dark childhood impressions, points the reader toward an understanding
of her that goes beyond idealization.

Dorothea admits to Will that the art in Rome seems
"a consecration of ugliness" in which "the feeling is
often low and brutal" (chap. 22):

At first when I enter a room where the walls are covered with
frescoes, or with rare pictures, I feel a kind of awe—like a child
present at great ceremonies where there are grand robes and
processions; I feel myself in the presence of some higher life
than my own. But when I begin to examine the pictures one
by one, the life goes out of them, or else is something violent
and strange to me. (Chap. 21)

These comments grow out of Dorothea's feeling that in
Rome, where "the past of a whole hemisphere seems
moving in funeral procession with strange ancestral
images." (chap. 20). The "dream-like strangeness of
her bridal life" is heightened by "this stupendous
fragmentariness":

[23] *The Great Tradtion,* p. 75.

Ruins and basilicas, palaces and colossi, set in the midst of a sordid present, where all that was living and warm-blooded seemed sunk in the deep degeneracy of a superstition divorced from reverence; the dimmer but yet eager Titanic life gazing and struggling on walls and ceilings; the long vistas of white forms whose marble eyes seemed to hold the monotonous light of an alien world: all this vast wreck of ambitious ideals, sensuous and spiritual, mixed confusedly with the signs of breathing forgetfulness and degradation, at first jarred with an electric shock, and then urged themselves on her with that ache belonging to a glut of confused ideas which check the flow of emotion. Forms both pale and glowing took possession of her young sense, and fixed themselves in her memory even when she was not thinking of them, preparing strange associations which remained through her after-years. (Chap. 21)

Barbara Hardy comments that there is a "reaction to sensuality" implied in these impressions of Rome.[24] I agree, and would add that these impressions revive and represent the primal scene. Dorothea is like "a child present at great ceremonies" who sees "something violent and strange" (just as later, when Will tells her about his parents and his past, she is "like a child seeing a drama for the first time" (chap. 37).

Dorothea's "feeling of desolation" in the presence of the "ancestral images" in Rome is like that of the child in the epigraph to chapter 21:

> A child forsaken, waking suddenly
> Whose gaze afeard on all things round doth rove,
> And seeth only that it cannot see
> The meeting eyes of love.

Her "forlorn weariness" alternates with "inward fits of anger and repulsion"—not clearly aimed at Casaubon, but experienced in great confusion. She defends against

[24] *The Appropriate Form* (London, 1964), pp. 126-27.

her anger by reversing it onto herself: "the mental act that was struggling forth into clearness was a self-accusing cry." When the reversal is effective, she lapses again into "forlorn weariness."

It may be instructive to pause at this point to compare George Eliot's handling of this material with that in earlier novels. In *Romola* the presentation of Florence may affect the reader as Rome affects Dorothea. But Romola stands marble-like and remote from the sordid life of the city. Revulsion is projected onto Dino, who sees Florence, and particularly his father's ambition, as a nightmare of sensuality. The latent connection between Romola's quest and Dino's revulsion does not mesh with the manifest treatment of the heroine, whose flights from Florence and dutiful returns are awkwardly manipulated and idealized. In *Felix Holt* the manifest treatment of Esther's moral growth is not isolated from primal material. Her father's story of passion and struggle makes a big change in her life. But her response to the disclosed secret is moralized, while revulsion is projected onto Felix and Harold. In *Middlemarch* the heroine is allowed to confront "strange ancestral images" and to react to them as "something violent and strange." The result is a tremendously enriched character. The author seems to be ready to confront again, through Dorothea, anger that emerged in the presentation of Maggie.

On the manifest level, Dorothea's feelings are accounted for by the obvious shortcomings of Casaubon, and particularly by his failure as a scholar to live up to her expectations. But the description of her growing disillusionment with Casaubon as husband and scholar comes *after* the allusion to her "fits of anger and repulsion," which is juxtaposed to her impressions of Rome. The emphasis on primal images implies that Dorothea's marriage to "a sort of father" is the fulfillment of an Oedipal fantasy which revives frightening and disgusting impressions of sexuality. The emotional response to the primal scene is repressed along with the memory (or fantasy) of it. But marriage to "a sort of father" brings these feelings and a veiled primal scene back to consciousness.

George Eliot's exploration of Casaubon's character, which requires a dramatic shift from Dorothea's view of the marriage to that of her equally disappointed husband,[25] serves many purposes. It checks the reader's sympathy with Dorothea while it reflects the author's freedom to step back from her heroine. It also functions defensively and expressively. Ostensibly, Casaubon is contrasted not only with Dorothea's expectations, but also with her ardor:

It is an uneasy lot at best, to be what we call highly taught and yet not to enjoy: to be present at this great spectacle of life and never to be liberated from a small hungry shivering self— never to be fully possessed by the glory we behold, never to have our consciousness rapturously transformed into the vividness of a thought, the ardour of a passion, the energy of an action, but always to be scholarly and uninspired, ambitious and timid, scrupulous and dimsighted. (Chap. 29)

In this description, Leavis senses "something adverting us that Dorothea isn't far away"[26]—by which he seems to mean that the pity for Casaubon implies unqualified praise of Dorothea. It's true that if we change the whole

[25] For a thorough discussion of this shift in perspective as it exemplifies the function of the narrator in *Middlemarch* see Knoepflmacher, *Laughter and Despair*, pp. 185-88.

[26] *The Great Tradition*, p. 65.

passage to a positive statement, it expresses Dorothea's ideal. But it also bases that ideal in a need "to be liberated from a small hungry shivering self." Dorothea is indeed not far away, but the connection we see is not what Leavis seems to have in mind. Her character contains not only the ardor which seeks outlets in thought and action, but also the fears and denials which, if allowed to take over completely, could produce a Casaubon. Thus the relationship between the two characters is not a simple contrast.

Casaubon's stiff behavior provides grounds for Dorothea's responses to him and thus disguises some-what the Oedipal component in her disillusionment. We are told that her disappointment with her husband's scholarly endeavors would have "remained longer un-felt" if he had "held her hands between his and listened with the delight of tenderness and understanding to all the little histories which made up her experience, and would have given her the same sort of intimacy in return, so that the past life of each could be included in their mutual knowledge and affection" (chap. 20). In-stead, Casaubon finds Dorothea's manifestations of af-fection "crude and startling." The fact that he does not encourage her to "pour forth her girlish and womanly feeling" is being emphasized in this passage, but it is of interest that we have seen little sign of these tendencies in her. It is as though she has just discovered them in herself. Before this it has always been Dorothea who has found sensuality "crude and startling" (as in her response to the word "fond" and her reaction to art). Thus her choice of husband confronts her with her own attitude toward sexuality in a more inflexible form.

Casaubon's scholarly inadequacies bear a similar relation to traits in Dorothea's character. Before her marriage she is bent on "regulating life"; she longs for "some command of money" to reorder her uncle's estate, and would have liked to organize his papers. She can't bear the chaotic mixture of sensual and ideal she sees in Rome, or the chaos of being a victim of her own feelings. She has a "strange fascination" with the money she feels is owing to Will Ladislaw, and is preoccupied with finding ways to dispose of her money, improve the world, and elevate her life. These compulsive aims are magnified in Casaubon. His anality is expressed in the imagery of dark tunnels and labyrinths and also in his actions. He does not hoard money, he hoards notations. His pamphlets, in which he "deposited small monumental records," are connected with his capacity for "severe self-restraint" (chap. 29). He may not have an enthusiastic soul, but "these minor monumental productions were always exciting" to him, even though "digestion was made difficult by the interference of citations." He keeps his documents "in pigeonholes," and hurtful criticism of his work in a little locked drawer. He sees only by the light of his own taper "stuck before him" as he collects his specimens (chap. 20). He regards other people only as possible sources of criticism, and relates to them only in terms of "acquitting himself and acting with propriety" (chap. 29).

We are meant to admire Dorothea's capacity to extend sympathy to Casaubon, and we do—especially since her sympathy, unlike Esther's for Mrs. Transome, involves a fairly thorough awareness of his faults. George Eliot is likewise to be admired for her success in turning the reader's sympathy toward Casaubon. He is the ultimate embodiment of a disavowed aspect of her-

self which came to light in the character of Silas
Marner. But the awareness that developed in the fantasy setting of that unique work is not integrated into
the author's realistic vision until *Middlemarch*. Placed
beside the similar father-figures in *Romola* (Bardo and
Baldassarre), Casaubon provides a measure of the author's growth toward self-acceptance and self-awareness. When asked about her source for the character of
Casaubon, George Eliot pointed to her own heart.[27] She
would not label his traits "anal" or "compulsive" as I
have here, but she acknowledges as her own the fears
behind his anality. Anal concerns abound in *Middlemarch,* and when they are more openly avowed, as in old
Mr. Featherstone's hoarding of money or Joshua Rigg
Featherstone's blatant passion for gold,[28] they receive
very harsh treatment. But Casaubon embodies, in his
awfulness, the same aims only slightly disguised, so
that through him a critical light is cast on all the ambitions in the novel—including the idealistic ones.

Casaubon's "small hungry shivering self" also embodies oral aims rather confusedly mixed with anal. He
hopes to find in Dorothea "a soft fence against the
world" until he finds implied criticism in her words and
she becomes a "personification of that shallow world
which surrounds the ill-appreciated or desponding author" (chap. 20). He "needed soothing" but shrank from
the implied judgment of pity. He is "lost among small
closets and winding stairs" where there is no sunlight,

[27] Haight, p. 450.
[28] See chap. 53: "The one joy after which his soul thirsted was to
have a money-changer's shop on a much frequented quay, to have
locks all round him of which he held the keys, and to look sublimely
cool as he handled the breeding coins . . ."

no "wide opening," and we can see him as imprisoned in the womb, unborn. He has "become indifferent to the sunlight"—does not possess the desire or energy to be born. His low vitality and ultimate death represent the self-destruction that results from succumbing to fear of life. Only death, which after the first cruel grasp "may come to fold us in his arms as our mother did," can soothe him (chap. 42).

Again, Dorothea is not far away. Her response to Casaubon's proposal of marriage reveals the passive aim behind her active idealism. After sobbing on her knees, unable to pray, she has a "rush of solemn emotion in which thoughts became vague and images floated uncertainly" and she "cast herself, with a childlike sense of reclining, in the lap of a divine consciousness which sustained her own" (chap. 5). We are to think of her reclining in the lap of God, but we also think of Casaubon's and, at the deepest level, a mother's lap. The "floating" and being "sustained" combine with the "childlike sense of reclining" to suggest passive oneness with the mother—oral bliss. The unfulfilled need for such oneness is apparent in Dorothea's thoughts after her marriage:

The clear heights where she expected to walk in full communion had become difficult to see even in her imagination; the delicious repose of the soul on a complete superior had been shaken into uneasy effort and alarmed with dim presentiment. When would the days begin of that active wifely devotion which was to strengthen her husband's life and exalt her own? (Chap. 28)

This "delicious repose," like the "reclining" and "floating" images, and the "warm flood," into which her resolves melt, combine with later images of babies and pregnancy to connect Dorothea with Casaubon's intra-uterine state.[29]

When we first see Dorothea at Lowick after the wedding journey there is no activity for her, and she has to keep contact "with a manifold pregnant existence" by means of "inward vision" alone, "painfully" (chap. 28). During the quarrel over Will's letter which leads to Casaubon's first heart attack, Dorothea's "pity, that 'newborn babe' which was by-and-by to rule many a storm within her," is overcome by anger (chap. 29). Instead of "reclining" we find Dorothea saying to Casaubon, "Can you lean on me, dear?" She is imprisoned in a tomb (or womb) with Casaubon, but she struggles against it. She originally thought it would be wonderful to assist Casaubon in his efforts to "reconstruct a past world" (chap. 2). She hoped that he could deliver her from the walled-in maze of her girlish ignorance. In Rome, however, she finds the past that Casaubon is trying to piece together revolting. And upon their return to Lowick she begins to see that Casaubon's knowledge simply leads her into another walled-in maze:

How was it that in the weeks since her marriage, Dorothea had not distinctly observed but felt with a stifling depression, that the large vistas and wide fresh air which she had dreamed of finding in her husband's mind were replaced by anterooms

[29] See chap. 48, in which Dorothea rejects sorting out Casaubon's parerga as "food for a theory which was already withered in the birth like an elfin child." This image of a withered embryo relates back to Dorothea's feeling on returning from Rome to Lowick that "every object was withering and shrinking away from her" (chap. 28). It is also elaborated in the person of Featherstone's illegitimate son (through whom he plans to get "gratification inside his coffin," chap. 34), a son who resembles a frog and is considered a "monstruosity" by Featherstone's family (ch. 41).

and winding passages which seemed to lead nowhither? (Chap. 20)

Where she expected to find the "sea," she finds instead an "enclosed basin."

Dorothea, unlike Casaubon, does possess the desire and the energy to be born. She has not grown indifferent to the sunlight. But in order to be born, to find the way out of her womb-tomb, she must somehow recover the past in order to release the energy bound up in repression. She seems to have no memories of her parents and almost none of her childhood, as if, as Will suggests, she had had no childhood (chap. 22). If the blank of her past is the result of repression, as one would guess, then her interest in the past—like Esther Lyon's—represents a desire to fill in that blank and integrate the past with her present life. Her marriage to a "sort of father" revives what Will calls the "vision of Hades" she must have had in childhood. But such contact with the blank of her past does not, as it did for Esther, result in a sudden (and unconvincing) release from her limitations. As Dorothea begins to see "that she was to live more and more in a virtual tomb, where there was the apparatus of a ghastly labour producing what would never see the light," she also begins to hunger for "a fuller sort of companionship" and "objects who could be dear to her, and to whom she could be dear" (chap. 48). But her desire for a fuller life is hampered by fear.

One thing Dorothea fears is the helplessness she associates with the feminine role. Her comment about the puppy offered her by Sir James sums up her estimate of the accepted feminine role and suggests her fear of it as well:

"It is painful to me to see these creatures that are bred merely as pets," said Dorothea, whose opinion was forming itself that very moment (as opinions will) under the heat of irritation.

"Oh, why?" said Sir James, as they walked forward.

"I believe all the petting that is given them does not make them happy. They are too helpless: their lives are too frail. A weasel or a mouse that gets its own living is more interesting. I like to think that the animals about us have souls something like our own, and either carry on their own little affairs or can be companions to us, like Monk here. Those creatures are parasitic." (Chap. 3)

This view of pets as "helpless" and "frail" as well as uninteresting coincides exactly with the Victorian woman's role which is ironically disparaged throughout the novel. In order to escape such helplessness, Dorothea aspires to the "provinces of masculine knowledge" (chap. 7). She chooses a husband she thinks "above" her "in judgment and in all knowledge," hoping to "become wise and strong in his strength and wisdom" (chap. 21). But this hope reveals the passive and somewhat parasitic aim behind her longing to do some useful work in the world. Her rejection of feminine concerns (she gives up ornaments much more easily than horseback riding) and her wish to subject herself to some great man in order to "become wise and strong in his strength and wisdom" do not save her from the helplessness she fears. Instead, her masculine ideal blinds her to her own needs.

The "stifling depression" that results from Dorothea's subjection to Casaubon is accompanied, we are told, by "the first stirring of a pitying tenderness fed by the realities of his lot and not by her own dreams" (chap. 21). The manifest message is that her pity marks the beginning of her moral growth. She has been guilty, the narrator implies, of "moral stupidity, taking the world as an udder to feed our supreme selves" (chap. 21). The udder image integrates the manifest emphasis with the oral passivity just described. But it is not so much the stirring of pity as it is the collapse of Dorothea's masculine ideal which may allow her to grow and emerge from her "virtual tomb."

When Dorothea sees Casaubon's inadequacies, the fear of helplessness behind her masculine ideal emerges. Her "ideas and resolves seemed like melting ice floating and lost in the warm flood of which they had been but another form. She was humiliated to find herself a mere victim of feeling, as if she could know nothing except through that medium . . . " (chap. 20). Thus, like Romola after a similar disillusionment, Dorothea is not long in forming a second ideal self-image as a defense against the chaos of her emotions—especially the rebellious anger she most fears. "Devotedness" is "so necessary a part of her mental life" that she must recover it: "Permanent rebellion, the disorder of a life without some loving reverent resolve, was not possible to her . . ." (chap. 20). Thus her "pitying tenderness," that newborn babe that will rule her, combines with her oral needs to become an ideal of mothering (or rescuing). With Casaubon she has little success, since he can't bear pity. But her "strong desire to rescue" finds other objects. She rescues Mr. Farebrother from his "chance-gotten money" by giving him the Lowick living (chap. 50). When Lydgate becomes the object of scandal, Dorothea's "yearning to give relief" meets with resistance in the form of her masculine protectors—her uncle, her brother-in-law, and even Mr. Farebrother. As a result, Dorothea's "emotions were imprisoned" and the "idea of some active good within her reach, 'haunted her like a passion' " (chap. 76). Her thoughts of Lydgate, which are connected not only to her own marriage troubles, but also to the painful recollection of his wife's relationship to "some one else," are "like a drama to her" (chap. 76).

Dorothea's imprisoned emotions can be released only through her attempts to give relief. Thus Lydgate's response to her sympathy is a vicarious gratification of the wish to find a "reclining" oral bliss (see pp. 161-162 above): "he gave himself up, for the first time in his life, to the exquisite sense of leaning entirely on a generous sympathy . . . " (chap. 76). But the triangular "drama" which energizes Dorothea's thoughts about Lydgate suggests that her urge to rescue and the orality behind it are regressive transformations of Oedipal interests.

The culmination of these acts and images is in Dorothea's anguished self-confrontation after her interruption of an intimate scene between Rosamond and Will. She "lay on the bare floor . . . while her grand woman's frame was shaken by sobs as if she had been a despairing child" (chap. 80). Her mental state is presented by this image:

> There were two images—two living forms that tore her heart in two, as if it had been the heart of a mother who seems to see her child divided by the sword, and presses one bleeding half to her breast while her gaze goes forth in agony towards the half which is carried away by the lying woman that has never known the mother's pang. (Chap. 80)

Dorothea has at this point become the mother whose child, Will, is "divided by the sword." It is also her own heart that is cut in two as she sobs like a "despairing child." She is both mother and child—the mothering satisfying oral needs through identification with the child (just as her "yearning to give relief" to Lydgate expresses her own need for rescue and relief). And once again it is an Oedipal triangle which leads to this response.

There is more to be said about this scene, and about Dorothea's relationship to Will Ladislaw. First it is necessary to see that Dorothea, failing to find a rescuer, reverses the situation and becomes one; failing to find oral bliss, she tries to provide it through mothering. On the manifest level it is stressed that her helping of others is now based on a clearer, more realistic view of other selves than she was capable of before her unhappy marriage. And this could be easily accepted, but for a simultaneous overemphasis on the nobility of Dorothea's self-subduing acts which suggests not only a reaction-formation against aggressive impulses, but also the uncritical participation of the author in Dorothea's intense need to "give relief." It is not difficult to find evidence of this need in George Eliot's life. It is clearly stated in her response to condolences after the death of Thornton Lewes:

Thanks for your tender words. It has cut deeper than I expected—that he is gone and I can never make him feel my love any more. Just now all else seems trivial compared with the powers of delighting and soothing a heart that is in need.[30]

George Eliot's primary contact with her fellow humans was through her novels, which, in spite of her avowal of realistic rather than idealistic aims, clearly function as attempts to rescue her readers. But such evidence is less significant for our understanding of *Middlemarch* than the latent pattern that emerges in the novel as a context for the need to "give relief."

The pattern of Oedipal disappointment, depression,

[30] Haight, p. 419, quoting *Letters*, V, 60-61.

and self-reproach which gives rise to Dorothea's motherly rescuing efforts deserves special notice here because it offers a clue to the peculiarly idealized self-denial at the center of all the novels we are considering. In "Mourning and Melancholia" Freud traces the self-reproaches of depressed patients back to "reproaches against a loved object" (which in all of these novels turns out to be the father and sometimes also, in a more disguised way, the mother).[31] When the original object choice is undermined by some injury or disappointment, resentment and even hate are aroused. But such feelings are unacceptable until they are transformed into self-hate. The reversal of hate onto the self is accomplished by a "regression from object cathexis to the still narcissistic phase of the libido" whereby the ego identifies itself with the abandoned object, and by a partial regression to the stage of sadism, whereby the super-ego takes up the reproaches against the object and turns them against the ego. Thus the outstanding feature of melancholia is "dissatisfaction with the self on moral grounds."

In both Maggie and Dorothea we find all the elements of this pattern, and one of the crucial indications of George Eliot's growth between *The Mill on the Floss* and *Middlemarch* lies in the new resolution she finds for Dorothea. Maggie's death is akin to suicide:—just before the flood she wonders, yearning, how long it will be before death comes (VII, v).—Her end reflects Freud's observation that the ego can kill itself when the animosity relating to an object is launched against the self with overwhelming force. Dorothea's life with Casaubon is presented as a kind of death, and at one point it

[31] *Standard Edition,* XIV, 248-49.

seems that Dorothea's end will be all too similar to Maggie's. When she is asked to decide whether her commitment to Casaubon's wishes will extend beyond his death, she stands "at the door of the tomb" (chap. 48) like Maggie "at the entrance of the chill dark cavern" (VII, v). Her answer seems to be "yes." Refusing him "would be like crushing that bruised heart," and she cannot so "smite" him. She is compelled by "compassion," which at this point amounts to identification, and by the idealization of self-denial which prevents anger and resentment from crushing her father-figure husband.

But even though George Eliot could not allow Dorothea to defy the ideal of self-denial at this point, she spares her from making a commitment to death by killing Casaubon before he gets his answer. Dorothea's inability to "smite the stricken soul that entreated hers" is called "weakness," but in an approving tone. The author seems to identify here with Dorothea's self-denial, and also with the need for it as a defense against sadistic impulses. At the same time, however, she has been carefully preparing for a distinctly new resolution to the pattern.

A successful refutation of Leavis's charge that Dorothea gives us "Maggie's case again" will have to show that Dorothea develops a degree of self-knowledge greater than any implied in her disillusionment with Casaubon or her mothering (rescuing) ideal. If we look very closely at the stages of her relationship to Will Ladislaw, we see that her self-knowledge does grow, even if so slowly that a twentieth-century reader would like to shake her, and that she moves away from her ideal self-image toward self-acceptance.

When Will first meets Dorothea he concludes, in spite of his enthusiasm for her Aeolian harp voice, that "there could be no sort of passion in a girl who would marry Casaubon" (chap. 9). There does not seem to have been much change when, hundreds of pages later, Lydgate wonders if Dorothea could have any other sort of passion for a man than the "heroic hallucination" which led her to Casaubon (chap. 76). But Dorothea is repeatedly described in terms of passion—her first, the passion for knowledge, and consequently, the passion for rescuing: the desire to rescue Lydgate "haunted her like a passion" (chap. 76). We are obviously going to be wondering about her passion (even if we are encouraged only to admire or identify with it).

Until Casaubon's death Dorothea is unaware of any feeling for Will Ladislaw beyond the friendly or motherly feelings she can approve of. If her rejection of sensuality and her resulting tendency toward blindness to what is obvious to others had not been carefully laid out, her density would indeed be simply unbelievable. As it is, Dorothea's denial of her own sensuality and sexuality is believable as being basic to both of her successive ideal images.

At Lowick she finds herself struggling "out of a nightmare in which every object was withering and shrinking away from her," *until* she focuses on the miniature of Will's grandmother. She identifies with the "woman who had known some difficulty about marriage" and the face gradually becomes Will's face, "with that gaze which tells her on whom it falls that she is too interesting for the slightest movement of her eyelid to pass unnoticed and uninterpreted." Dorothea's dreary oppression gives way to a "pleasant glow"—but the glow is dispelled by guilt before it reaches her conscious interpretation. She immediately has an "irresistible impulse to go and see her husband and inquire if she could do anything for him" (chap. 28).

Because of the suppression of her love for Will, Dorothea cannot understand or even seem to remember Casaubon's jealousy of him, although by this time she is supposedly aware of her husband's needs and "no longer struggling against the perception of facts" (chap. 37). She feels, once she knows about Will's parentage, a "sympathy that grew to agitation" (chap. 37). As a result, we are told, "Dorothea's mind was innocently at work towards the further embitterment of her husband." Her "peculiar fascination" with Will's parentage and prior right to what would become her property develops into the disguised vehicle for her denied passion and for unconscious aggression against her husband-father. She plans to convince Mr. Casaubon of the need to rectify the past: "The vision of all this seemed to Dorothea like a sudden letting in of daylight, waking her from her previous stupidity and incurious self-absorbed ignorance . . . " (chap. 37). Her "young ardour is set brooding over the conception of a prompt deed," and her blindness seems to her like waking, because there is passion for Will finding its way to the surface, however indirectly or disguisedly. At the same time her "peculiar" fascination involves, by means of identification with Will, setting things right with her own past.

Dorothea's self-awareness makes a significant step forward when she has her first occasion for jealousy. She unexpectedly finds Will in Rosamond's company and leaves preoccupied with "the sudden sense that there would be a sort of deception in her voluntarily allowing any further intercourse between herself and Will which she was unable to mention to her husband" (chap. 43). In addition to that "explicit" thought was a "vague discomfort" as she found herself thinking "with some wonder that Will Ladislaw was passing his time with Mrs. Lydgate in her husband's absence." She questions her own similar actions and feels "confusedly unhappy, and the image of Will which had been so clear to her before was mysteriously spoiled." Her "vague discomfort" is not felt as jealousy until she repeats the scene of discovery much later.

Another triangular situation involving jealousy further increases Dorothea's self-knowledge. When she learns of the codicil to Casaubon's will forbidding her to marry Will Ladislaw she is aware of a "violent shock of repulsion from her departed husband," a repulsion which seems to cancel the guilt which forbids her to admit her longing for Will. At the same time she feels "a sudden strange yearning of heart towards Will Ladislaw." She "might have compared her experience at that moment to the vague, alarmed consciousness that her life was taking on a new form, that she was undergoing a metamorphosis in which memory would not adjust itself to the stirring of new organs" (chap. 50). The sexual image of "new organs" gives greater clarity to Dorothea's strange longing, but only for the reader. Dorothea, herself, is far from being able to accept this "state of convulsive change" all at once:

It had never before entered her mind that he could, under any circumstances, be her lover: conceive the effect of the sudden revelation that another had thought of him in that light—that perhaps he himself had been conscious of such a possibility. (Chap. 50)

Dorothea's return to Lowick as a widow is motivated by
her longing to see Will. She admits to herself, while she
explains aloud to her dead husband why she cannot
continue his unfinished work, that "underneath and
through it all there was always the deep longing which
really determined her to come to Lowick" (chap. 54).
She supposes that she longs to see him simply because
his was the one "human gaze which rested upon her
with choice and beseeching" in her past life, and ration-
alizes her feeling into faithfulness to the past.

After her first farewell scene with Will, Dorothea
wonders at the "passionate grief" she gives vent to.
Since "their delight in speaking to each other" is "forever
ended," she can allow herself to dwell on it "without
inward check" (chap. 55). She does not recognize her
feeling as love, but she is described as "a freshly-opened
passion-flower," and she "took the little oval picture in
her palm and made a bed for it there, and leaned her
cheek upon it, as if that would soothe the creatures who
had suffered unjust condemnation" (chap. 55). The creatures represented by the portrait of Will's grandmother
include not only Will, but also herself. If it seems odd
that we are asked not to criticize the "woman's tenderness" expressed in this act, it is probably because the
image of making a bed for the miniature is more sexual
than motherly. The narrator's request, here, seems to
guide the reader away from awareness of the sexual
implications of Dorothea's act. But the author wants us
to be—like herself—ahead of Dorothea, who still does
not acknowledge the nature of what she feels:

She did not know then that it was Love who had come to her
briefly, as in a dream before awaking, with the hues of morning on his wings—that it was Love to whom she was sobbing

her farewell as his image was banished by the blameless rigour of irresistible day. (Chap. 55)

The little which Dorothea does acknowledge is based on the certainty that it is "forever ended."

In reference to this passage, Barbara Hardy makes an objection which can be seen as an extension of Leavis's:

The appropriate comment seems to be that at this point in the story she should have known. There are some Victorian novels in which it might seem captious not to accept such a lack of self-knowledge but *Middlemarch* is not one of them. George Eliot spends a fair amount of energy criticizing Dorothea's ignorance and short-sightedness but here remains romantically identified with this innocence.[32]

It seems to me that Dorothea's lack of self-knowledge is, on the contrary, adequately accounted for as the inevitable result of her fear and rejection of sensuality, and of her rejection of the actual self which hides behind her ideal self.[33] The kind of person who is driven by an ideal self-image has developed it as a substitute for self-confidence, which he desperately lacks. Such a person, and Dorothea is one, could not possibly tolerate the vulnerability of loving without the greatest assurance of reciprocation, especially with the added fear of sexuality we see in Dorothea.

That George Eliot is deeply involved in Dorothea, and particularly in her idealized self, is beyond argument. But she is more deeply involved, although perhaps unconsciously, in driving her character toward greater self-knowledge. The painstaking detail which leads up

32 *The Appropriate Form*, p. 124.

33 See Karen Horney, *Neurosis and Human Growth* (New York, 1950), chap. 1, passim. Horney's analysis of neurosis has been helpful in my study of *Middlemarch*, and I find no conflict between the insights it leads to and the insights founded on strict Freudian theory.

to Dorothea's discovery of her passion to herself, the gradual emergence and submergence, the repetition of farewell scenes and discovery scenes, are a measure of the author's reluctance and determination. George Eliot must be deeply involved with the need to break through resistances, or she would not submit her character to the heavy blow which alone will break down her defenses.

George Eliot prepares us for that blow by building up the gossip about Will and Rosamond. Mrs. Cadwallader reports the gossip to Dorothea just before her second farewell scene with Will. Dorothea insists to herself that the gossip is not true, but she can't help remembering the day she found Will with Mrs. Lydgate (chap. 62). While her feelings are alternating between "anger with Will and the passionate defense of him," she unexpectedly finds him in her uncle's library. They both feel "something that suppressed utterance," but it is Will who finally declares his love for Dorothea. He first complains that what he cares "more for than anything else" is "absolutely forbidden" to him, and Dorothea feels "crowded" by images "which left the sickening certainty that Will was referring to Mrs. Lydgate." "But why sickening?" Dorothea wonders, still not knowing that she loves. Only when Will's last words make it clear that he loves her, does Dorothea have the basis of courage she needs to admit to herself her own feelings.

With Will's declaration that he is "in danger of forgetting everything else" but her, Dorothea experiences "the first sense of loving and being loved":

It was as if some hard icy pressure had melted, and her consciousness had room to expand: her past was come back to her with larger interpretation. The joy was not the less—

perhaps it was the more complete just then—because of the irrevocable parting; for there was no reproach, no contemptuous wonder to imagine in any eye or from any lips. (Chap. 62)

Dorothea's joy still depends upon their parting; she can accept her feelings only if there is no possibility of acting on them. Her longings are not yet openly sensual; knowing she is loved does not change her character in one miraculous blow. She wished she "could but have given him the money, and made things easier for him!"—these "were the longings that came back the most persistently." Her motherly self concentrates on Will as "in need of help and at a disadvantage with the world" and "there came always the vision of that unfittingness of any closer relation between them which lay in the opinion of every one connected with her":

She felt to the full all the imperativeness of the motives which urged Will's conduct. How could he dream of her defying the barrier that her husband had placed between them?—how could she ever say to herself that she would defy it? (Chap. 62)

We know that her husband's testament is not Dorothea's only barrier to union with Will. Her unrecognized, repressed fears are projected onto Casaubon's recorded suspicions. Dorothea's mothering self-image is still in control, and from this point on criticisms and rumors about Will only give "more tenacity to her affection" and "more enthusiasm to her clinging thought" (chap. 77). But when she once again finds Will and Rosamond together, this time with Rosamond in a state of "flushed tearfulness" and Will clasping her hands and speaking "with low-toned fervour," Dorothea drives away "animated" by "self-possessed energy":

It was as if she had drunk a great draught of scorn that stimulatd her beyond the susceptibility to other feelings. She had seen something so far below her belief, that her emotions rushed back from it and made an excited throng without an object. She needed something active to turn her excitement out upon. She felt power to walk and work for a day, without meat or drink. (Chap. 77)

This tremendous energy and excitement do not emerge from Dorothea's idealized self, but from a self that has long been suppressed.

Dorothea's discovery relates back to her marriage to "a sort of father" and the "violent and strange" images of Rome, as well as to the "vague discomfort" of her first intrusion on Will and Rosamond. This time the return of the repressed brings her face to face with herself. After her vision of herself as a mother whose child has been "divided by the sword," Dorothea finally confronts her passion:

Here, with the nearness of an answering smile, here within the vibrating bond of mutual speech, was the bright creature whom she had trusted—who had come to her like the spirit of morning visiting the dim vault where she sat as the bride of a worn out life: and now, with a full consciousness which had never awakened before, she stretched out her arms towards him and cried with bitter cries that their nearness was a parting vision: she discovered her passion to herself in the unshrinking utterance of despair. (Chap. 80)

Now Dorothea is *not* content that this is a parting, rather than a uniting. At the same time she admits to other forbidden feelings: to pride (her "lost woman's pride of reigning in his memory"), and anger and jealousy:

And there, aloof, yet persistently with her, moving wherever she moved, was the Will Ladislaw who was a changed belief exhausted of hope, a detected illusion—no, a living man to-

wards whom there could not yet struggle any wail of regret-
ful pity, from the midst of scorn and indignation and jealous
offended pride. The fire of Dorothea's anger was not easily
spent, and it flamed out in fitful returns of spurning reproach.
. . . Why had he brought his cheap regard and his lip-born
words to her who had nothing paltry to give in exchange? . . .
Why had he not stayed among the crowd of whom she asked
nothing—but only prayed that they might be less contemptible? (Chap. 80)

When Will at this point is seen as a "living man" rather
than as Dorothea's child or Dorothea's hope, a significant change has occurred. Her identification with him
has been part of the pattern of melancholia (discussed
above, pp. 167-169) and thus closely connected with the
Oedipal conflict, which in this case, gives rise to the pattern. Will has not been presented as essentially an Oedipal object, but the aspects of taboo (embodied in Casaubon's will) and competition have the effect of reviving
that repressed conflict. Dorothea's interruption of Rosamond and Will thus revives emotions related to the
primal scene ("something so far below her belief") and
her confrontation of those emotions becomes a means
of release from the defensive pattern established to deal
with them. Instead of identifying with Will and turning
anger against herself, Dorothea unleashes her "scorn
and indignation and jealous offended pride" against the
"living man" present to her mind.

Freud refers to the pattern of melancholia not as a
system[34] but as a process—"the work performed in
melancholia" can, like mourning, gradually loosen the
fixation of the libido to the object. But apparently in
order for this to happen the ambivalence toward the
object must at times break through the defensive rever-

[34] "Mourning and Melancholia," *Standard Edition,* XIV, 257.

sal of hate onto the self. Then "by disparaging the object, denigrating it, even as it were by slaying it" the fixation and the pattern can be overcome. When this happens the ego has triumphed (though what the ego has surmounted remains hidden from it) and the energy that has been "bound" suddenly becomes available. Thus Dorothea's emotions "made an excited throng without an object" and she "felt power to walk and work for a day, without meat or drink." The regression to narcissistic identification and orality seems to be reversed, so that when Dorothea's anger has at last been focused on an object and expressed (if only in the solitude of her own room), she is ready to exchange her heavy mourning dress for something new. The sorrow that remains with her belongs to the loss of a loved object who is no longer identified either with her own ego or with the past conflict from which she has emerged.

Ultimately, when Dorothea comes to the question of what she should do now, she takes up her mothering self-image once again. She attempts to "clutch" her pain and "compel it to silence" and to focus once more on "the objects of her rescue." She resolves to "see and save Rosamond," but her resolve is not strong enough to carry her through the whole scene. At the beginning Dorothea's mothering softens Rosamond. Then Dorothea's own suffering begins to surface in tones "like a low cry from some suffering creature in the darkness." Her self-image gives way, and she begins to dread "speaking as if she herself were perfection addressing error." This dread is new—Dorothea has often spoken this way without dread or awareness. Now she admits "I am weak":

The waves of her own sorrow, from out of which she was struggling to save another, rushed over Dorothea with conquering force. (Chap. 81)

Then "the two women clasped each other as if they had been in shipwreck," and we wonder who is rescuing whom? On the manifest level we are asked to admire "the saving influence of a noble nature, the divine efficacy of rescue that may lie in a self-subduing act of fellowship" (chap. 82). And certainly Dorothea's return to Rosamond is both difficult and admirable. But at a less conscious level we see that for Dorothea (and indirectly for Rosamond), it is not the self-subduing as much as the self-expression that is saving. When Dorothea's resolve is conquered by emotion, her suffering moves Rosamond to tell the truth. Rosamond, who had been "inwardly wrapping her soul in cold reserve," responds to new impulses which "delivered her soul" (chap. 81). The suggestion of birth in "delivered" is reinforced by the surrounding water imagery. The waves "rushed over Dorothea"—not drowning her, but bringing her out of her imprisonment.

This birth is not immediately apparent in the final scene between Dorothea and Will. We find that Dorothea still has "a great deal of superflous strength" and feels "throbbing excitement like an alarm" when she is about to receive Will (chap. 83). Nevertheless, she is "afraid of her own emotion" and looks "as if there were a spell upon her, keeping her motionless and hindering her from unclasping her hands, while some intense, grave yearning was imprisoned within her eyes." Her fear is not new, but her acknowledgement of it is new. We are told that "what she was least conscious of was her own body: she was thinking of what was likely to be in Will's mind, and of the hard feelings that others had had about him." This denial of body consciousness is not encouraging, and neither are her first words, which fit the old image: "You acted as I should have expected you to act." Eventually her control wavers, however, and Will begins to give way "to his own feeling in the evidence of hers" and to express the despair he has just gone through. Dorothea's control breaks down a bit more after Will kisses her hand, and she is "distressed" at her "confusion."

At this point the storm outside takes over the expression of growing emotion, while Dorothea and Will watch "the evergreens which were being tossed, and were showing the pale underside of their leaves against the blackening sky." This projection of emotion onto the storm is only partly an avoidance; it is also clearly expressive, since the characters, too, have begun to show "the pale undersides of their leaves" to one another.

In the midst of the storm Dorothea again takes refuge in her mothering image, and her moralizing finally makes Will angry:

"It is cruel of you to speak in that way—as if there were any comfort. You may see beyond the misery of it, but I don't. It is unkind—it is throwing back my love for you as if it were a trifle, to speak in that way in the face of the fact. We can never be married."

"Some time—we might," said Dorothea, in a trembling voice.

Will's anger is a relief, to me at least, but his petulant complaint following Dorothea's trembling suggestion that they might someday be married, is grating: " 'When?' said Will, bitterly. 'What is the use of counting on any success of mine?' " It is clear that if Dorothea and

Will are to get together, it will have to be her doing.
Dorothea is no longer debating, we are told; she simply
cannot say what she wants to say. But after Will's
exasperated "Good-bye," she finally comes through:

> "Oh, I cannot bear it—my heart will break," said Dorothea,
> starting from her seat, the flood of her young passion bearing
> down all the obstructions which had kept her silent . . . (Chap.
> 83)

The "flood of her young passion," like the "waves of her
own sorrow," conquers. "All the obstructions which had
kept her silent," not only Casaubon's will and the opinion of others, but also her own fears and resolves, are
finally overcome by passion for a man, a man her own
age who offers no illusion of greatness or knowledge or
superiority.

Once we have observed the minutely differentiated
stages of Dorothea's movement toward self-knowledge
and self-acceptance, it is impossible to object, as Leavis
does, that when Dorothea's search for truth turns into
passion for Will Ladislaw, we have "Maggie's case a-
gain" with the confusions, the unacceptable valuations,
and the daydream self-indulgence.[35] There is no doubt
that George Eliot identifies a great deal with Dorothea
in the sense of expressing through her many of the
writer's deepest fears and desires as well as ideals. But
every time Dorothea's defensive "innocence" or defensive motherliness is offered over-sympathetically rather than critically, the author takes Dorothea one
more step toward emergence from those defenses.
Where does this push toward life and maturity come
from, if not from the same George Eliot who has, ac-

[35] *The Great Tradition,* p. 77.

cording to Leavis, "the genius that is self-knowledge and a rare order of maturity"?[36]

In this lengthy scrutiny of the stages of Dorothea's relationship with Will, I have relied heavily on the manifest content in order to stress the degree of deliberateness and awareness we can impute to the author. It may not have been necessary to go so far in meeting Leavis's criticism on its own terms. But in this case it was useful to show the hesitancy and the almost imperceptible progress toward self-acceptance and away from regression, defense, and denial. The final stage of awareness in Dorothea is certainly not complete. Her passion for Will is accepted partly in oral and anal terms. She has her own fortune to offer him, and continues to revert to the idea of his need and the injustices done to him, as a basis for indentification with him. But essentially he is neither her child nor her father nor her own ego—but a "living man" who cannot be chosen out of self-denial or idealism. Thus Dorothea's choice is a clear step toward acceptance of adult sexuality and toward acceptance of a more real than ideal self. She may be "childlike" in the moment when her passion breaks through her defenses, but the child is undeveloped ego rather than incongruous innocence, and that undeveloped ego affirms life—as a sadistically distorted superego cannot.

II

To a certain extent the success of George Eliot's attempt to express her "new awareness of the value of life" through Dorothea depends upon her portrayal of Will Ladislaw. Unfortunately, many of the criticisms leveled

[36] Ibid., p. 76.

at Will are justifiable. The most injurious criticism comes
from Barbara Hardy, who objects that the "complete-
ness" of *Middlemarch* is marred by the "restricted treatment of sex . . . in Dorothea's relation to Ladislaw."[37] She
establishes very convincingly that George Eliot's "reti-
cence" about the Casaubon marriage, "because it is not
silence, is compatible with a truthful and complete
account of what is was like for Dorothea to be married
to Casaubon, and what it was like for Casaubon to
be married to Dorothea."[38] She finds Will Ladislaw
lacking as the antithesis to Casaubon in a "structural
relationship" which, though flawed, marks *Middlemarch*
as part of a common fictional pattern which she calls the
"rescue into love."[39] In all such novels, "the sexual rescue—from an old man, a woman, a sterile aesthete— has
social implications. The rescuer is something of the
Noble Savage and something of the Outsider, representing not only personal passion and fertility but the
new blood needed and feared by the old establishment."
Ladislaw, according to her analysis, "completes and answers these social implications," but "as a noble savage
he is a little fragile."[40] He falls short as the rescuer and
sexually potent foil to the sterile Casaubon; and this,
Mrs. Hardy claims, is because in the relationship of Will
and Dorothea, "George Eliot is dealing with a situation
which she cannot even name," and is unwilling "even to
suggest" the passions involved.

Mrs. Hardy's criticism throws light on Casaubon's
sexual inadequacy, but in doing so ignores some aspects
of the change going on in Dorothea. She seems to

[37] *The Appropriate Form,* p. 121.

[38] Ibid., p. 108.

[39] Ibid., pp. 121-22.

[40] Ibid., p. 123.

conclude that if George Eliot were able to be honest on the subject, she would have Dorothea marry a trooper after Casaubon's death (as Henry James's Constantius suggests).[41] This is to mistake Dorothea's intermittent glimpses of her true feelings at the point of Casaubon's death for total sexual liberation and complete change of character. It is true that the imagery presents Will as representing to Dorothea the way out of her dark tomb. But it is not a simple contrast of virility versus impotence which so marks him. He is an opportunity for Dorothea to approach the sexuality she has previously denied while maintaining some of her defenses and pared-down ideals. Dorothea's urge to rescue demands a needy object, not a trooper, and suggests a pattern of "rescue into love" in which Will is not only rescuer but also the object of rescue, and as such is an appropriate and psychologically plausible partner for Dorothea.

Will Ladislaw, like Dorothea, is immature in his attitude toward love and sexuality. His feeling for Dorothea is based on ambivalence, the hostile aspect of which is defended against by idealization. From the beginning of his relationship with her, Dorothea is Will's saint, his "soul's sovereign." When he sees her "looking in her plain dress of some thin woolen-white material, without a single ornament besides her wedding ring, as if she were under a vow to be different from all other women," he has "the unspeakable content in his soul of feeling that he was in the presence of a creature worthy to be perfectly loved" (chap. 37). He delights in "her thought as a pure home," the place where he finds his "highest estimate" (chap. 77). She is

[41] Ibid., p. 125.

the perfect "crystal" Will wants to see the light through.

George Eliot quite deliberately exposes the romantic exaggeration in Will's thoughts about Dorothea:

> She must have made some original romance for herself in this marriage. And if Mr. Casaubon had been a dragon who had carried her off to his lair with his talons simply and without legal forms, it would have been an unavoidable feat of heroism to release her and fall at her feet. (Chap. 21)

The fantasy of heroically rescuing Dorothea from a dragon is immediately given up; Casaubon "was something more unmanageable than a dragon: he was a benefactor with collective society at his back, and he was at that moment entering the room in all the unimpeachable correctness of his demeanour" (chap. 21). Instead of rescuing her, Will soon sees Dorothea as rescuing *him:*

> "You teach me better," said Will . . . "I have really sometimes been a perverse fellow," he went on, "but I never will again, if I can help it, do or say what you would disapprove."
>
> "That is very good of you," said Dorothea, with another open smile. "I shall have a little kingdom then, where I shall give laws." (Chap. 37)

Mrs. Hardy objects to the "romantic glow" in Will's relationship to Dorothea, apparently because it is "strikingly absent" from his other relations, particularly that with Rosamond.[42] She admires the hostile declaration of love for Dorothea that Will hurls at Rosamond:

> "I never had a *preference* for her, any more than I have a preference for breathing. No other woman exists by the side of her." (Chap. 78)

[42] Ibid., p. 121.

According to Mrs. Hardy, this exemplifies "George Eliot's psychological truthfulness at its best" while the "romantic glow" between Dorothea and Will "seems false."[43]

From my point of view, however, Will's harsh treatment of Rosamond is not inconsistent with his idealization of Dorothea: one attitude is not psychologically true and the other false. The idealization is a familiar aspect of romantic love which has historical roots in Courtly Love and psychological roots in ambivalence toward the mother. Richard A. Koenigsberg, in his application of Freudian concepts to the conventions of courtly love,[44] relates the idealization of the Lady to the Oedipus complex:

> The child's knowledge of the infidelity of the mother, in the classical description of the Oedipus complex, is bound up with his discovery of her participation in sexuality. This discovery is anxiety-provoking, because it leads to excessive excitation, and hostility-generating, because it reveals the mother's infidelity in its most concrete and irrevocable form. Concurrent with this disappointment and serving as a defense against it, is the tendency to regard the mother as "a personification of impeccable moral purity," and to deny her involvement in sexual activities.

The extreme idealization of the Lady, in light of the above, may be understood as a way of coming to terms with unconscious hostility and disappointment. In attempting to repress his ambivalence, in attempting to keep his love pure and untainted by contradictory emotions, the Courtly Lover conceived of the Lady as a faultless creature. If the speeches seem hollow to us now, unnecessarily exaggerated and melodramatic, it is likely that an increase in psychological sophistication lies beneath our change in taste. The Courtly Lover pro-

43 Ibid., p. 128.
44 "Culture and Unconscious Fantasy: Observations on Courtly Love," *Psychoanalytic Review* 54 (1967): 36-49.

tests too much. Beneath the echoes of praise we detect the voice of hostility, the secret loathing for an unfaithful and castrated creature.[45]

I have quoted this explanation at length because I wish to show the truth and complexity of George Eliot's portrayal of Will. Will's idealization of Dorothea is exaggerated, it is defensive, and the hostility which he unleashes on Rosamond is an integral part of his attitude which breaks through repression when he is threatened with the loss of his ideal relationship.

Will's relationship to the theme of rescue can also be understood with the help of Koenigsberg's interpretation of courtly love:

In Courtly Love, the desire to rescue the beloved in order to preserve her virtue, as described by Freud, is transformed into the phantasy of being rescued *by* the beloved. The love affair provides confirmation of the worth of a man's character rather than the opportunity to salvage the character of a woman.[46]

Will's vow to try to live up to Dorothea's high estimate of him fits into this pattern, as does his need for recognition:

He was rather impatient under that open ardent goodwill, which he saw was her usual state of feeling. The remote worship of a woman throned out of their reach plays a great part in men's lives, but in most cases the worshipper longs for some queenly recognition, some approving sign by which his soul's sovereign may cheer him without descending from her high place. That was precisely what Will wanted. (Chap. 22)

The Oedipal origins of Will's romantic idealization are expressed in the novel in several ways. He has

[45] Ibid., pp. 45-46.
[46] Ibid., p. 43.

chosen not only a married woman, but the young wife of an uncle who took over the support of his mother and himself when his father died. He is, like the courtly lover, "attempting to recreate the conditions of the Oedipal triangle, to reconstruct in adult reality the basic trauma of his childhood," and "to deny the original victory by the father."[47] The existence of Casaubon as Dorothea's husband is a necessary condition of Will's romantic love: "What others might have called the futility of his passion, made an additional delight for his imagination: he was conscious of a generous movement, and of verifying in his own experience that higher love-poetry which had charmed his fancy" (chap. 47). He is jealous of Casaubon, but does not hope for his removal:

It may seem strange, but it is the fact, that the ordinary vulgar vision of which Mr. Casaubon suspected him—namely, that Dorothea might become a widow, and that the interest he had established in her mind might turn into acceptance of him as a husband—had no tempting, arresting power over him; he did not live in the scenery of such an event, and follow it out, as we all do with that imagined "otherwise" which is our practical heaven. It was not only that he was unwilling to entertain thoughts which could be accused of baseness, and was already uneasy in the sense that he had to justify himself from the charge of ingratitude—the latent consciousness of many other barriers between himself and Dorothea besides the existence of her husband, had helped to turn away his imagination from speculating on what might befall Mr. Casaubon. And there were yet other reasons. Will, we know, could not bear the thought of any flaw appearing in his crystal: he was at once exasperated and delighted by the calm freedom with which Dorothea looked at him and spoke to him, and there was something so exquisite in thinking of her

47 Ibid., p. 45.

just as she was, that he could not long for a change which must somehow change her. (Chap. 47)

Will has many, *too* many, reasons for accepting Casaubon as an immovable obstacle. It *does* "seem strange," from a rational point of view, that Will does not imagine that Dorothea might become a widow and himself her husband. From the psychoanalytic point of view, however, the need for the injured third party is comprehensible.

When the injured third party is removed by the death of Casaubon, Will is compelled to exaggerate the "other barriers" between himself and Dorothea, and finally to leave Middlemarch:

> Until now Will had never fully seen the chasm between himself and Dorothea—until now that he was come to the brink of it, and saw her on the other side. He began, not without some inward rage, to think of going away from the neighbourhood: it would be impossible for him to show any further interest in Dorothea without subjecting himself to disagreeable imputations—perhaps even in her mind, which others might try to poison.
> "We are for ever divided," said Will. "I might as well be at Rome; she would be no further from me." (Chap. 51)

Will, up until this point, has not cared about the opinion of other people, has even enjoyed shocking them; nor has he cared much about his lack of money. All this suddenly changes, but Will does not immediately leave Middlemarch, despite his need to reestablish distance between himself and Dorothea. He also needs, in order to maintain his self-esteem, some "expression of strong feeling from Dorothea" (chap. 54). But instead of the declaration of love he is seeking, Dorothea offers him the miniature of his grandmother, a gesture which turns out to be a prefiguring of the "inherited blot" which Bulstrode will reveal.

Dorothea's availability as a love object destroys an equilibrium and produces anxiety. The anxiety grows out of an increase in sexual temptation which is experienced as a threat,[48] and brings back the repressed ambivalence resulting from the child's discovery of the mother's sexuality. In the novel the return of the repressed is expressed in Will's relationship with Rosamond, and Bulstrode's revelation of Will's "inherited blot." On the manifest level the disclosure of Will Ladislaw's connection with Bulstrode seems a bit artificial, but at the level of latent meaning the "inherited blot" represents the childhood conflict which underlies the conditions of Will's object choice, an Oedipal conflict symbolized in the story of Bulstrode's past. Before Will's confrontation with Bulstrode, he has already been questioned by Raffles about his parents, and "felt as if he had had dirt cast on him amidst shouts of scorn" (chap. 60). He insists to Bulstrode that his mother "was a very generous, honourable woman," while he feels anger, suspicion, and repugnance toward any connection with the man: "It seemed like the fluctuations of a dream—as if the action begun by that loud bloated

[48] Ibid., p. 42. "The interdependence of 'distance' and desire represented the need to recreate the love-object in the image of a remote, hardly accessible creature. To be an Oedipal substitute, it was necessary that the Lady be represented as a superior, infallible person, approachable in only the most delicate, tactful fashion. In addition, distance was necessitated by the forbidden nature of the love-object. An increase in familiarity destroyed desire, not only because it prevented idealization, but because it led to an increase in sexual temptation which was experienced as a threat and which, if intensified beyond a certain point, resulted in the complete repression of affect toward the woman . . . "

stranger were being carried on by this pale-eyed sickly-looking piece of respectability, whose subdued tone and glib formality of speech were at this moment almost as repulsive to him as their remembered contrast" (chap. 61).

Will violently refuses Bulstrode's offer of money, money which would have removed the barrier of poverty between himself and Dorothea. He was "strongly possessed with passionate rebellion against this inherited blot":

> "My unblemished honour is important to me. It is important to me to have no stain on my birth and connections. And now I find there is a stain which I can't help. My mother felt it, and tried to keep as clear of it as she could, and so will I. You shall keep your ill-gotten money. . . . It ought to lie with a man's self that he is a gentleman." (Chap. 61)

Bulstrode's revelations to Will are "discoveries which he would have been glad to conjure back into darkness." Their connection with Will's repressed memories and feelings is quite clear.[49]

This return of the repressed is accompanied by outbursts of hostility. Will is brutal with Bulstrode. And in spite of his concern for his honor and Dorothea's good opinion, he is causing ugly rumors by dallying with Rosamond. His resurgent hostility seems to create the situation which will provide an outlet. "He had felt no bond beforehand" to Rosamond, so that after Dorothea has discovered them together, Will feels himself "blame-

---

[49] Ibid., p. 45 Koenigsberg sees the courtly lover's "denial of the importance of one's heredity" (p. 44) as a representation of the child's "wish to be father of himself," an aspect of the rescue fantasy. It is closely related to the idealization of the lady, an extension of the child's view of the mother as "a personification of impeccable moral purity" which defends against the discovery of her participation in sexuality.

less" toward the woman who has "spoiled the ideal treasure of his life." He has "a horrible inclination to stay and shatter Rosamond with his anger," and snatches up her words "as if they were reptiles to be throttled and flung off" (chap. 78).

Rosamond, the speaker of those "reptile" words, "recoils." In terms of Will's hitherto repressed hostility and its origin in the discovery of the mother's sexuality, the snake imagery reflects the child's fear of castration. The mother's sexuality is not only resented as infidelity, but also feared because her lack of a penis implies the possible loss of the child's. It may seem contradictory for Will to see Rosamond in phallic terms, and then himself as "maimed" (chap. 83), going through life with his "limbs lopped off" (chap. 82) as a result of her evil influence. But the snakes represent a denial of the woman's anatomy: they are attempts to replace the penis, and thus to insure against the possiblity of castration, which nevertheless is feared.[50]

After his rage has been expressed, Will's self-knowledge has increased. The return of the repressed seems to provide an opportunity for a more mature concept of love. When Will learns from Rosamond's note that she has told Dorothea of his love for her, he feels like a "man who has escaped from wreck by night and stands on unknown ground in the darkness" (chap. 82). Yet he doubts that he and Dorothea will recover their "world apart where the sunshine fell on tall white lilies, where no evil lurked."

Will does not conquer his old attitudes without Doro-

[50] Freud, "Medusa's Head," *Standard Edition*, XVIII, 273. In this discussion Freud finds a "confirmation of the technical rule according to which a multiplication of penis symbols signifies castration."

thea's help. She is the one who prevents him from going away at the end. But her break-through is urged upon her by Will's anger at obstacles which he now sees as "petty accidents" and by his refusal to admire and accept Dorothea's motherly, moralistic reassurance that his life "need not be maimed" (chap. 83).

I second Reva Stump's argument that Will's reaction here shows that "the chivalrous attitude no longer holds any charm" for him.[51] She claims that instead of the "romantic world of white lilies and sunshine" Dorothea and Will now look out at "a stormy, tumultuous world":

> The storm in this scene is more than a dramatic background for a correspondingly dramatic situation, and more than a mere symbol of the real world in contrast to the unreal world of lilies and sunshine. It is in itself such a brilliantly shocking revelation of the overwhelming forces at work in the real world that it arouses a sense of awe and mystery, thus cutting through to another level of reality where the fittingness of union between man and woman is to be measured against something more than appearances.[52]

Will's reponse to Dorothea's suggestion that they might be married sometime may sound petulant, as I have suggested, but it is also, as Reva Stump proposes, a realistic appraisal of his expectations:

Having once drifted into selling himself as a pen to the ineffectual Mr. Brooke, Ladislaw clearly does not entertain such a future. Now he stands before Dorothea, "rayless" at last, no longer a bright and sunny romantic hero whose credo is delight, but a man who having made a "sober calculation" knows that he "can count on nothing but a creeping lot." Perhaps Ladislaw has been reduced to something less than he

---

[51] *Movement and Vision in George Eliot's Novels* (Seattle, 1959), p. 210.
[52] Ibid., p. 209.

was in his formlessness when everyone speculated about how he would "turn out." Life has imposed its limitations on him and forced him down a certain path. But as a child in becoming a man becomes both something less and something more, so Ladislaw has become something more in the very process of taking on form. Dorothea has been for him a shaping influence. And she accepts him now, not as one who can take her "along the grandest path," but simply as the man she loves.[53]

Ultimately, the above defense of Will Ladislaw in terms of psychological truthfulness does not remove the possibility of finding him somewhat unsatisfactory—as most readers do. Ian Milner suggests that Ladislaw's inadequacies as a character—"His physical presence and distinct personality are faint"—may be explained by his possible origin in George Henry Lewes.[54] But U. C. Knoepflmacher's argument is more solidly based within the novel:

Will Ladislaw has always disturbed those readers of *Middlemarch* who, after the manner of Leslie Stephen, find the "young gentleman" to be "conspicuously unworthy of the affections of a Saint Theresa." But Dorothea is *not* a Saint Theresa, nor is her second marriage meant to be an ideal union of the "heart" and the "mind." If Ladislaw's unsatisfactoriness persists, this is so, not because of his unsuitability as Dorothea's husband, but because, as a character, he serves too many different roles in the novel's ideological scheme. As a physical foil to the weak-legged Casaubon, Ladislaw is portrayed as being young, vital, "a spirited horse"; as the intellectual foil to the blind "Bat of erudition" of Lowick, he is depicted as a "sunny" Ariel who can interpret history imaginatively and who can, above all, "read the idealistic in the real." Although Will can thus see in Dorothea an "ideal"

---

[53] Ibid., pp. 210-11.
[54] *The Structure of Values*, p. 82.

perceived neither by Casaubon nor by Lydgate, he is by no means an idealized figure himself.[55]

Will Ladislaw may have too much potential and not enough actual form, even in the end, but he is right for Dorothea because he needs her and because he values her.

The Fred Vincy-Mary Garth story, which parallels that of Will and Dorothea in some ways, avoids the depths of inner conflict we have just explored. Fred's need is a simplified version of Will's. Without Mary he would be lost: "I never shall be good for anything, Mary, if you will not say that you love me . . ." (chap. 14). His conscience depends on Mary's "decided notions as to what was admirable in character" and his efforts are to measure up to her standards. He does not seem to have any of Will's ambivalence toward women or toward his competitor and fatherly guide, Mr. Farebrother. His response to Farebrother's avowal of love for Mary is simple: " 'I could not be expected to give her up,' he said, after a moment's hesitation: 'it was not a case for any pretense of generosity.' " Likewise Farebrother's "fine" act in warning Fred that his gambling could result in losing Mary is a simplified and low-keyed version of Dorothea's self-subduing acts. He acts partly on principle, but mostly out of love for Mary and certain knowledge of her preference for Fred.

Mary has Dorothea's motherly inclinations, though she is no passionate rescuer: her love for Fred is more "maternal" than "girlish," and when Fred is sufficiently penitent she feels "an instantaneous pang, something like what a mother feels at the imagined sobs or cries of her naughty truant child, which may lose itself and get

[55] *Religious Humanism and the Victorian Novel* (Princeton, 1965), p. 96.

harm" (chap. 25). Mary's happy fate is partly the result of her good fortune in having parents who are both morally strong and extremely loving. These is no emptiness, no craving in her to necessitate the search for glory. She even seems to be so constituted that under no circumstances would she be prone to "longing for illimitable satisfactions" or to "loving heart beats and sobs after unattained goodness" (Prelude).

In a sense the simplifications and lowered intensity of the Fred-Mary story reflect the novel's movement away from the highly emotional and ambitious idealism of the Saint Theresa "Prelude." But this is only part of the picture. The restoration of parents here, while the main characters are all orphans, suggests that this somewhat idyllic plot constitutes the final stage of a family romance. The orphans are preoccupied with ideals and ambitions which veil unresolved Oedipal conflicts, while Fred and Mary, whose parents are present, seem almost to exist in a state of innocence. Fred's attachment to Mary is extremely similar to Godfrey Cass's love for Nancy Lammeter. But in Fred's case there is no lost mother to replace and no degrading secret marriage to hide. There are no demons to combat.[56] His moral growth is hindered somewhat by ineffective parents who must be replaced by Mary, Farebrother, and the Garths. And this is accomplished with a minimum of difficulty.

Mary's love for Fred is equally free of lurking doubts or overwhelming needs. If he becomes responsible and finds a vocation suited to his nature, she will accept him. In any event she is sustained by an adoring father who

[56] There is the "Green Dragon," of course, a highly domesticated version of demon.

is to her "the best man in the world" (chap. 86). Basically Mary is spared having to deal with the problem of
ambivalence toward the father which is so prominent in
most of *Middlemarch* and in preceding novels. At one
point, however, the author's unspent rage seems to
break in upon the wished-for family-romance reconciliation. When the dying Featherstone begs Mary to take
his gold and then throws his stick at her "with a hard
effort which was but impotence," Mary defies him: "I
will not let the close of your life soil the beginning of
mine" (chap. 33). This symbolic confrontation with Oedipal and anal dangers seems oddly incongruent with
the Fred-Mary idyll as a whole. The intensity of the
scene belongs to the latent content of the rest of the
novel, and Mary's defiant statement, with its startling
relevance to Dorothea's relation to Casaubon, seems
like an involuntary outburst on George Eliot's part.

Strangely enough neither this outburst nor the perfect wish-fulfillment of Mary's situation, which re-
stores and improves upon the author's lost past, seems
to reduce the effectiveness of the story. As Knoepflmacher justly observes, "the story of Mary's love for
and regeneration of Fred" is an idyll "which could easily
have degenerated into a mawkish homily on the powers
of true love and of practical, hard work"—but it doesn't:

It is a tribute to George Eliot's integrity and artistic skill that
this idyll is neither homily nor overdramatized wish-
fulfillment; though it encases her own idealism, it remains
perfectly compatible with the reality of a novel in which the
lives of most other characters are not crowned by a happy
ending.[57]

---

[57] *Laughter and Despair*, p. 177.

In my opinion the story of Fred and Mary "encases" George Eliot's idealism only in a very limited sense. Neither Fred nor Mary exhibits any of that high ambitious idealism which is built on repression. Thus their fate is not encompassed by the melancholy which stems from the inevitable failure of the neurotic "search for glory" and spreads through most of *Middlemarch*. Mary Garth's personality is in itself an antidote to melancholy. Her physical plainness with its "peculiar temptations and vices," her "shrewdness" with its "streak of satiric bitterness," her "truth-telling fairness," and her humor are expressions of the non-Dorothea in George Eliot's nature.

III

Henry James, who admired in Dorothea the "beautiful spirit" that Leavis deplored, and found in her "the great achievement of the book," regretted that her career was "not distinctly enough . . . the central one," and that Lydgate carried off the "lion's share" of attention. His personal preference for one central intelligence did not prevent him, however, from admiring "the balanced contrast between the two histories of Lydgate and Dorothea":

Each is a tale of matrimonial infelicity, but the conditions in each are so different and the circumstances so broadly opposed that the mind passes from one to the other with that supreme sense of the vastness and variety of human life, under aspects apparently similar, which it belongs only to the greatest novels to produce.[58]

The contrast is important, but to emphasize difference

[58] "George Eliot's *Middlemarch*," reprinted in Gordon S. Haight, ed., *A Century of George Eliot Criticism* (Boston, 1965), pp. 81-84.

and opposition, while relegating similarity to the level of appearances, is to lose a great deal. When my mind passes from Dorothea's story to Lydgate's it is with a sense of their original and fundamental similarity. The differences gain significance from this essential sameness, which is part of the artistry and vision that make *Middlemarch* a complex unity rather than an "indifferent whole."

Lydgate, like Dorothea, is not only an orphan, but an uncommon person. His appearance is a masculine version of hers: he has dark steady eyes, a deep sonorous voice, and a proud openness. He, too, is an "emotional creature," interested in reform and contemptuous of petty obstacles. Above all, Lydgate, like Dorothea, has ardor. His ardor is poured not into soul-hunger but into his work as a doctor. He is, for George Eliot, an "imagined otherwise," and so well imagined that his fate tells us a great deal about George Eliot's awareness and evaluation of the kind of change we see in Dorothea.

Lydgate's childhood vigor becomes ardor when, while he is still a lad, his quest for fresh reading brings him upon the anatomy section of an old cyclopedia (chap. 15). His eyes fall on a passage about the valves of the heart and "through this crevice came a sudden light" (the imagery reminds us of Dorothea).[59] His education had given him nothing beyond "a general sense of secrecy and obscenity in connection with his internal structure," but with his new light he imagines filling the "vast spaces blanked out of his sight by that wordy

[59] See above, p. 171: Dorothea's plan to rectify the injustices of Will's past "seemed to her like a sudden letting in of daylight" and her "young ardour is set brooding over the conception of a prompt deed" (chap. 37).

ignorance which he had supposed to be knowledge."
Again we are reminded of Dorothea's hope that greater
knowledge would fill in the blanks in her life.[60]

In an ironical tone George Eliot anticipates some objection to her intention of telling the story of an "intellectual passion.":

Is it due to excess of poetry or of stupidity that we are never
weary of describing what King James called a woman's
"makdom and her fairnesse," never weary of listening to the
twanging of the old Troubadour strings, and are comparatively uninterested in that other kind of "makdom and fairnesse"
which must be wooed with industrious thought and patient
renunciation of small desires? In the story of this passion, too,
the development varies: sometimes it is the glorious marriage,
sometimes frustration and final parting. And not seldom the
catastrophe is bound up with the other passion, sung by the
Troubadours. (Chap. 15)

This playful apology emphasizes, unconsciously perhaps, the importance of that "sense of secrecy and obscenity" which preceded Lydgate's passion for anatomy, and which, we are told (but cannot quite believe), left his imagination "quite unbiassed" on the subject. We *can* believe that Lydgate's success or failure in medicine will be "bound up with the other passion" especially if sexual passion is included in the "renunciation of small desires" necessary for wooing intellectual "makdom and fairnesse." But this does not seem to be the intended message. The undercurrent suggests that the two kinds of passion are "bound up" more directly than the ironist is willing to acknowledge.

[60] We are reminded as well of the blank in Esther's knowledge which
is replenished by Lyon's primal disclosures. See also, above, p. 93 in the
chapter on *Romola* where I discuss Fenichel's analysis of obsessive doubt
as "the instinctual conflict displaced to the intellectual field."

The most striking indication of this direct connection is the story of Lydgate's passion for an actress which immediately follows the ironic apology above. While still a student, Lydgate became infatuated with an actress who played the part of stabbing her lover (her husband in real life). His only relaxation from his studies was "to go and look at this woman." A "remote impersonal passion" for this dark-eyed beauty of soft cooing voice and sweet matronliness of form changed into "personal devotion, and tender thought of her lot" when one night she "veritably stabbed her husband" during the play. Suddenly, Lydgate found himself on the stage ("he hardly knew how") "making the acquaintance of his heroine by finding a contusion on her head and lifting her gently in his arms" (no mention of concern for the dead man). She was suspected of willful murder, but Lydgate "vehemently contended for her innocence" and became "madly anxious about her affection, and jealous lest any other man should win it."

After her release, Laure disappeared, and Lydgate imagined her "stricken by ever-wandering sorrow . . . and finding no faithful comforter." He finally found her again in a theater in Lyon[61] "looking more majestic than ever as a forsaken wife carrying her child in her arms." He resolved to ask her to marry him, recognizing that "he had two selves within him" which must "learn to accommodate each other." When he proposed, she rejected him and admitted that she purposely murdered her husband—not because of any great abuse, but be-

[61] See previous footnote. The resemblance between Rufus Lyon's disclosures to Esther and this forsaken wife and child is conspicuous. Unlike Lyon, Lydgate has the desire to accomodate both of the "two selves within him." But his disillusionment with Laure leads to repression of the libidinal self.

cause he wearied her, he was too fond, and wanted to live in Paris rather than in her country.

This story is a highly condensed expression of Oedipal wishes and the primal scene. Lydgate's initial role as a passive observer of Laure suggests the child's early fascination with the mysterious sexual activities of the parents. Laure represents the mother: she has not only the motherly qualities of "sweet matronliness" and "quietude," but a second role as "forsaken wife carrying her child in her arms." The original tenderness which turns to passionate love and jealousy, and the replacement of the murdered husband by a child, are expressions of Oedipal wishes. At the same time the stabbing represents a primal scene. Lydgate's insistent belief in Laure's innocence represents the child's denial, in response to that alarming scene, of the mother's sexuality and infidelity. His urge to rescue the mother is a regressive transformation of Oedipal desire. But Oedipal or oral, desire for the mother—"the divine cow" (chap. 16)—must be repressed after Laure confesses to murder.

Lydgate remembers Laure, and sees Rosamond as "her very opposite" (chap. 16). What he has lost sight of is that libidinal self whose needs have been partly repressed and partly sublimated through "the exercise of disciplined power" in medical research, where he seeks to "pierce the obscurity of . . . those invisible thoroughfares which are the first lurking-places of anguish, mania, and crime." His profession provides the "triumphant delight" of mastery and an opportunity to satisfy a mothering need through gentleness toward "the weak and suffering" (chap. 31). But Lydgate's unacknowledged needs and fears, like Dorothea's, produce blind spots which the narrator calls "spots of commonness."[62] He is attracted to qualities in Rosamond which add up to reassurances against the disgusting impurity and uncontrollable passion associated with Laure (the stabbing mother). Rosamond is "immaculately blond" with a "well trained" voice, "self-possessed grace" and refined manners. Best of all, he feels no "agitation" in regard to her, nothing suggesting the "madness" he felt for Laure, just aesthetic admiration:

Certainly, if falling in love had been at all in question, it would have been quite safe with a creature like Miss Vincy, who had just the kind of intelligence one would desire in a woman— polished, refined, docile, lending itself to finish in all the delicacies of life. . . . Lydgate felt sure that if ever he married, his wife would have that feminine radiance, that distinctive womanhood which must be classed with flowers and music, that sort of beauty which by its very nature was virtuous, being moulded only for pure and delicate joys. (Chap. 16)

In short, Lydgate's need for mastery (which seems to involve a regressive identification with the stabbing mother) demands a thoroughly domesticated object, the kind of creature bred merely as a pet that Dorothea abhors.

Thus, while Rosamond builds up her dream of a future with him, Lydgate goes home thinking "only in the second place" of her. After reading into the smallest hours, he relaxes:

As he threw down his book, stretched his legs towards the embers in the grate, and clasped his hands at the back of his head in that agreeable after-glow of excitement when thought

---

[62] There is some prejudice in this description, I think, since Dorothea's blind spots are generally regarded more as spots of *un*commonness.

lapses from examination of a specific object into a suffusive sense of its connections with all the rest of our existence— seems, as it were, to throw itself on its back after vigorous swimming and float with the repose of unexhausted strength—Lydgate felt a triumphant delight in his studies, and something like pity for those less lucky men who were not of his profession. (Chap. 16)

The "vigorous swimming," as Hilda Hulme points out, is "essentially a masculine and sexual image."[63] But it characterizes Lydgate's pleasure in research, not sex. The "after-glow," when thought seems to "float with the repose of unexhausted strength," is the second part of the swimming image, and it is only this passive repose which relates to the place reserved for woman in Lydgate's mind. He thinks that marriage to a strenuous woman like Dorothea would be "about as relaxing as going from your work to teach the second form, instead of reclining in a paradise" (chap. 10). And this idea of marriage, which is reminiscent of Dorothea's illusory hope of "reclining in the lap of a divine consciousness" (chap. 5), reveals a regressive need which betrays him.

Lydgate does not choose Rosamond as a mother in whom he can find passive bliss. In fact, he chooses her company partly because she has no motherly qualities. But when Rosamond's artificial graces break down, and for a moment she is as natural as a child, Lydgate's repressed needs emerge as a kind of mothering (not unlike Dorothea's). Rosamond's tears and "a certain helpless quivering" inspire a belief "that this sweet young creature depended on him for her joy," and Lydgate is mastered by his own "outrush of tender-

63 "The Language of the Novel: Imagery," in Hardy, *"Middlemarch": Critical Approaches*, pp. 87-124.

ness." He "put his arms around her, folding her gently and protectingly—he was used to being gentle with the weak and suffering" (chap. 31).

Thus Lydgate's intellectual ardor, like Dorothea's, is undermined by a choice based on repressed sexuality. But the influence of such repression on Lydgate's character and career gets even less notice from critics than Dorothea's. Jerome Thale, who recognizes the "repression and evasion"[64] of sexuality as a significant dimension of Dorothea's aspiration, does not see the parallel in Lydgate. In his terms "the major characters come to grief because they are too preoccupied with their aspirations to know themselves." This seems true enough. But only if the causality is reversed do we find a way to see the characters more clearly than they see themselves. They preoccupy themselves with their aspirations in order (unconsciously) to *avoid* knowing themselves—in order to maintain their repressions and evasions.

Lydgate's arrogance, "massive in its claims and benevolently contemptuous," and his tendency toward "fitful swerving of passion," are qualities which imply unrecognized needs and desires. Dorothea's inconsistency, we recall, was combined with more disguised arrogance: she was supposedly not "self-admiring," but her attitude of superiority was apparent in her puritanic toleration of Celia and in her wish that Will had stayed "among the crowd of whom she asked nothing, but only prayed that they might be less contemptible." This last expression is not far from Lydgate: "He would do a great deal for noodles, being sorry for them, and feeling quite sure that they could have no power over him . . . "

---

[64] *The Novels of George Eliot* (New York, 1959), p. 108.

(chap. 15). The need for supremacy, which is expressed as arrogance, is a reaction to basic anxiety and a constituent of what Karen Horney calls the "search for glory."[65] In Lydgate's case the anxiety stems from the wound to self-esteem implicit in Laure's rejection of his proposal—a wound which represents the child's sense of injury and loss when his Oedipal wishes are frustrated and his mother's infidelity is revealed. In Dorothea's case the derivation is hidden, but the "vision of Hades" Will senses in her past suggests an Oedipal injury parallel to Lydgate's.

Once engaged, Lydgate thinks that he has found "ideal happiness (of the kind known in Arabian Nights, in which you are invited to step from the labour and discord of the street into a paradise where everything is given to you and nothing claimed)" (chap. 36). His few moments of happiness with Rosamond resemble the "after-glow" of his pleasure in research, when he feels the "old delightful absorption in a far-reaching inquiry, while Rosamond played the quiet music which was as helpful to his meditation as the splash of an oar on the evening lake" (chap. 64). But when Rosamond's passive-aggressive schemes take the form of feminine dictation, the negative side of Lydgate's ambivalence emerges, and his anger threatens to overthrow his tenderness: "he was prepared to be indulgent towards feminine weakness, but not towards feminine dictation" (chap. 64).

In his afterthoughts, Lydgate always attempts to excuse Rosamond. He undergoes a disillusionment like

---

[65] *Neurosis and Human Growth*, pp. 19-35. Horney does not trace basic anxiety to Oedipal sources or primal scenes, but there is nothing in her theory which prevents one from doing so.

Dorothea's with Casaubon, and like Dorothea's, his mind is occupied not with understanding himself, but with making resolutions:

The first great disappointment had been borne: the tender devotedness and docile adoration of the ideal wife must be renounced, and life must be taken up on a lower stage of expectation, as it is by men who have lost their limbs. But the real wife had not only her claims, she had still a hold on his heart, and it was his intense desire that the hold should remain strong. In marriage, the certainty, "She will never love me much," is easier to bear than the fear, "I shall love her no more." Hence, after that outburst, his inward effort was entirely to excuse her, and to blame the hard circumstances which were partly his fault. (Chap. 64)

This passage bears a close resemblance to Dorothea's accommodation to her disappointing marriage with Casaubon, most significantly in the attempt to turn reproaches against the loved object back upon the self (see pp. 167-168 above). And like Dorothea's resolves, Lydgate's repeatedly give way to outbursts of anger.

At this point, however, Lydgate's masculine role becomes extremely significant as a determining factor in the resolution of his difficulties. George Eliot points out his advantage of having, as a man, a kind of work which places "external calls on his judgment and sympathies" and draws him "out of himself" (chap. 66). His work thus counteracts his personal cares. But it also allows him to avoid painful self-knowledge. Dorothea, who finds no outlet in work, is constantly confronted with the unfulfilled needs which push her toward self-acceptance. Her gradual increase in self-knowledge depends heavily on the jealousy she feels when she finds Will and Rosamond together. But Lydgate never suspects or thinks of such matters. His pride is invested primarily in his work.

The difference between masculine and feminine roles has another effect as well. Because Dorothea's masculine ideal never approaches realization, she has little to lose by accommodating herself to Casaubon through self-denial and submission. Her superego can readily adopt such aims when the first ideal collapses. But Lydgate is actively engaged in pursuing his idealized ambition. His fear of ceasing to love Rosamond, and the deeper fear of releasing the full force of his anger against her, urge him to reproach himself and make concessions. But such concessions inevitably undermine his aspirations and thus conflict with his superego ideals.

As a result, Lydgate's inner conflict has a crippling effect, rather than a growthful one. When he begins to see the disparity between his idealized view of Rosamond and the "real wife" he has to deal with, Lydgate inwardly sees Laure while looking at Rosamond and wonders "Would *she* kill me because I wearied her?" (chap. 58). His quick conclusion, "It is the way with all women," is checked by the memory of Dorothea. But Lydgate does not come to terms with the fear associated with Laure or accept the fact that, like her, Rosamond "meant to live as she pleased" (chap. 31) and has the strength to do so. He continues to try to "excuse her," and in doing so he deceives himself about her: "He wished to excuse everything in her if he could—but it was inevitable that in that excusing mood he should think of her as if she were an animal of another and feebler species" (chap. 65).

Lydgate's dilemma is not altered, as Dorothea's was, by the death of his spouse. His self-deception about Rosamond makes him blame "hard circumstances" for his misery, and he preoccupies himself with money probems as he once had with his aspirations—still as a means of maintaining his repressions. But when Lydgate finds himself "enveloped" by Bulstrode's character, we see another instance (compare Will Ladislaw's contact with Bulstrode, p. 192) in which the portrayal of Bulstrode acts as a vehicle for the return of the repressed.

In the account of Lydgate's passion for Laure there was no indication of any guilt feeling on Lydgate's part. Much later he does feel something like guilt in relation to money. But it is only in the story of Bulstrode's past life, and in his subsequent murder of Raffles, that money and Oedipal guilt come together. The manifest coincidence which brings Lydgate to Bulstrode at the fatal moment is one of those coincidences pointing to a significant latent connection.

Bulstrode, like Dorothea, Lydgate, and Ladislaw, is an orphan. When he was a young banker's clerk and a lay preacher of a dissenting congregation, he became an intimate of the Dunkirks, the richest family in the congregation.[66] At the death of a subordinate partner, Mr. Dunkirk made Bulstrode his confidential accountant; and at the death of Mr. Dunkirk, Bulstrode married his widow. Her son was already dead, and Bulstrode concealed from her his discovery that her daughter was still alive. Thus at the death of the mother, Bulstrode inherited the family fortune.

Before the death of Mr. Dunkirk, Bulstrode discovered that the family business profited from the reception of stolen goods, and he rationalized his complicity into harmony with his belief that Providence had special

[66] The pre-Dunkirk part of Bulstrode's past is remarkably similar to the past that Silas Marner leaves behind.

work for him to do. Before his marriage to the widow, he rationalized his lie about her daughter in the same way. And for thirty years afterward he experienced conspicuous prosperity, which he interpreted as God's sanction of his deeds. But then Raffles appears, the only person who knows how he came by his money. Raffles had been paid for "keeping silence and carrying himself away," and his sudden reappearance brings back the past like "the terrible irruption of a new sense overburthening the feeble being" of Bulstrode (chap. 61). When Raffles proves unmanageable, Bulstrode is prepared to defy him and face ignominy, but the old man's illness makes putting him out of the way too easy to resist.

There are two equally interesting approaches to Bulstrode's guilt. The first is its relationship to money. The deaths involved in Bulstrode's rise to power are seen by him as "striking dispositions," signs of God's approval. But we are told that long before his acquaintance with the Dunkirks, the young lay preacher had had "striking experience in conviction of sin and sense of pardon" (chap. 61). The Oedipal nature of Bulstrode's original guilt is suggested by his marrige to a mother-figure (which involves displacing her husband and her daughter) and confirmed by his murder of the old man who knows his secret. His misdealings with money are like the criminality arising from a sense of guilt—transgressions which follow rather than precede his guilt.[67] His lie to Mrs. Dunkirk about her daughter, ostensibly motivated by money, can also be seen as unconsciously motivated by a desire to eliminate all competition for the mother's love.[68] The more obvious

[67] Freud, "Character Types," *Standard Edition*, XIV, 332-33.
[68] "The Sexual Enlightenment of Children," ibid., XII, p. 305. Freud

motive is not arbitrarily chosen, however; it indicates an anal fixation strong enough to determine the regressive form that repressed Oedipal desire will take.

Bulstrode's insistence that the money is for God's work (himself "being indifferent to it," chap. 61), like the insistence that Mr. Dunkirk's business had "no pettiness or dinginess to give suggestions of shame," is an attempt to disguise even the anal motive. This disguise resembles similar disclaimers by the narrator regarding other characters. Rosamond "had no wicked plots, nothing sordid or mercenary; in fact, she never thought of money except as something necessary which other people would always provide" (chap. 27). Lydgate "had an ideal of life which made this subservience of conduct to the gaining of small sums thoroughly hateful to him" (chap. 18). In fact, the "deliberate pursuit of small gains" was "altogether repulsive to him." Just as Bulstrode's obvious rationalization makes us see these other denials more clearly, so also the Oedipal guilt behind his anality illuminates the connection between money and repressed Oedipal desires in all the other characters of *Middlemarch* (and earlier novels), and in the author's unconscious fantasies.

A second interesting approach to Bulstrode's guilt is through its relationship to his "search for glory." The narrative emphasis falls not on Bulstrode's crime, but on the activity of his conscience. His relationship to money and power does not differ greatly from Featherstone's except in the fact that he is "a man who believes in

---

describes lies which "proceed from the influence of an excessive love motive," including one case in which "we are confronted with one of those extremely common cases of persistence of early anal eroticism in the later erotic life."

something else than his own greed" and thus "has necessarily a conscience or standard to which he more or
less adapts himself" (chap. 61). Bulstrode's beliefs, we
are assured, are not consciously affected "for the sake
of gulling the world"—they are simply not as strong as
his desires. And this, the narrator proposes, "is a process which shows itself occasionally in us all" (chap. 61).
Instead of conscience restraining desire, conscience
translates desire into acceptable terms. Bulstrode's
"search for glory" takes the form of getting "as much
power as possible," and with the help of his conscience
this ambition is transformed into "self-abhorrence and
exaltation of God's cause" (chap. 61). The "self-
abhorrence" is not simply a theoretic denial of pride. It
is based on a deep sense of being "sinful and nought" (see
Karen Horney's description of the self-hate behind the
pride system).[69] Bulstrode's sense of being "sinful and
nought" creates an "immense need of being something
important and predominating" (chap. 61). He needs
money for power, and power in order to be a "predominating" agent in furthering God's cause: "He believed
without effort in the peculiar work of grace within him,
and in the signs that God intended him for special
instrumentality" (chap. 61). When his special instrumentality is threatened by Raffles, his belief that Providence intends his rescue makes even murder possible.
And after he has effectively murdered Raffles, his
conscience is "soothed by the enfolding wing of secrecy,
which seemed just then like an angel sent down for his
relief" (chap. 70).

Bulstrode's secret is soon pieced together by the
Middlemarchers, however, and the ensuing scandal is

[69] *Neurosis and Human Growth,* pp. 110-54.

one of those "currents" which touches all of the characters in the novel in various ways and moves toward
the conclusion. The narrator's exploration of the inter-
relationship of needs, desires, conscience, and pride in
Bulstrode provides the context for a series of climactic
scenes in which pride breaks down and "direct fellow-
feeling" (chap. 61) repairs some of its damages. Lydgate
is the character most directly affected by the Bulstrode
scandal. His rage, when he recognizes the "blight" that
has fallen on him through his indebtedness to Bulstrode, is manifestly attributed to the frustration of his
"honourable amibition" (chap. 73). But the latent connection between Bulstrode's Oedipal guilt and Lydgate's gives even greater significance to his outburst.
He rages in solitude, fearing that the sight of Rosamond
might "exasperate him and make him behave unwar-
rantably." And for the first time he looks at his marriage as an "unmitigated calamity." But his soul-
searching, as always, turns toward professional rather
than personal concerns. He admits that his indebtedness to Bulstrode stopped him from investigating
Raffle's death as thoroughly as he would otherwise
have done. And his "agonized struggles of wounded
honour and pride" thrust Rosamond out of his
thoughts and produce an "obstinate resolve" to explain
himself to no one.

Thus Lydgate is utterly rebellious and isolated by his
pride until Dorothea sends for him in order to declare
her belief in his innocence. Her understanding and
sharing of that grief which comes from trying and
failing to "lead a higher life than the common" does not
make a new man of Lydgate. His life cannot be made
"quite whole and well again," as she hopes. But there is

more than the obvious significance to the fact that "it was something very new and strange in his life that these few words of trust from a woman should be so much to him" (chap. 76). In response to "the searching tenderness of her woman's tones," he "gave himself up, for the first time in his life, to the exquisite sense of leaning entirely on a generous sympathy, without any check of proud reserve" (chap. 76).

In terms of Lydgate's fate, there is no great reward or release following this breakdown of pride. He accepts "his narrowed lot with sad resignation" (chap. 82). His experience with Dorothea (as the narrator predicts in chap. 10) has modified "his opinion as to the most excellent things in woman." It has also healed somewhat the old wound inflicted by Laure, so that the two separate selves within him can begin to come together again.

Rosamond's pride is subjected to a more severe influence in the scene following Lydgate's with Dorothea. Will Ladislaw feels blighted by his connection with Rosamond, just as Lydgate did by his connection with Bulstrode. After Dorothea's interruption, Will has "a horrible inclination to stay and shatter Rosamond with his anger" (chap. 78). For Rosamond the exposure to Will's fury is a totally new experience:

She had no sense of chill resolute repulsion, or reticent self-justification such as she had known under Lydgate's most stormy displeasure: all her sensibility was turned into a bewildering novelty of pain; she felt a new terrified recoil under a lash never experienced before. What another nature felt in opposition to her own was being burnt and bitten into her consciousness. (Chap. 78)

Will's rage, though just as clearly an agent for good as

Dorothea's trusting compassion, is presented with apologies: "Let it be forgiven to Will that he had no such movement of pity. . . . He knew that he was cruel, but he had no relenting in him yet." George Eliot, I think, is not relenting, either, despite the note of apology. Rosamond seems almost to have been created with this harsh scene in mind, not as an end in itself but as a preparation for the scene of mutual rescue that follows after Dorothea confronts her own rage and "jealous offended pride."

The collapse of Rosamond's egoistic dream world balances the collapse of Dorothea's idealistic dream world. When pride breaks down between these two and they clasp each other "as if they had been in a shipwreck" we have something quite different from Lucy's forgiveness of Maggie, or Romola's mothering of Tessa, or Esther's soothing of Mrs. Transome. Here the acceptance, the comforting, and the embrace are mutual. The dichotomy between the egoist and the altruist seems to vanish when Dorothea's mothering gives way to "her own sorrow" and Rosamond's self-enclosed pain "involuntarily" gives way to a comforting gesture. The embrace between two suffering women reflects and also transcends earlier mother-daughter reconciliations by erasing—as least momentarily—the parent-child distinction.

In terms of George Eliot's resolution of the conflicts originally expressed through Maggie and recast in Dorothea, this transcendence has deep significance. It is made possible by the fragmentary explorations of parent-child relationships in *Silas Marner, Romola,* and *Felix Holt,* where the hidden wounds of childhood are exposed and allowed to heal, and where the destructive feelings associated with those wounds are released, bringing with them lost aspects of the self.

The Author's Introduction to *Felix Holt* ends with a parable:

> The poets have told us of a dolorous enchanted forest in the under world. The thorn-bushes there, and the thick-barked stems, have human histories hidden in them; the power of unuttered cries dwells in the passionless-seeming branches, and the red warm blood is darkly feeding the quivering nerves of a sleepless memory that watches through all dreams. These things are a parable.

George Eliot's exploration of her private "under world" becomes, through her creations, a process of self-discovery for all of us to share. The dark power of "unuttered cries" to destroy life diminishes when those cries are uttered, freeing the "red warm blood" for loving contact with the upper world. In *Middlemarch* these things are no longer a parable.

Conclusion

In the preceding chapters I have concentrated largely on details relevant to each novel's central conflicts. At this point I will retrace the emergent pattern and relate it to the author's self-discovery.

The father-daughter relationship, which is a conspicuous element in each of the novels and points to an unresolved Oedipus complex, proves to be less central than originally expected. Instead, oral and anal needs predominate. It is not possible to determine whether they appear as regressive responses to Oedipal frustration or as fixations which persist into and complicate the Oedipal situation. But our analysis bears out repeatedly that Oedipal relationships have a distinctly pre-Oedipal quality, while oral and anal needs dominate the latent content.

Maggie's dilemma in *The Mill on the Floss* is the first full expression of George Eliot's pain and conflict. The conflict, apart from the incest taboo, can be seen as a "separation conflict," in which a frustrated desire for passive oral-dependency is pitted against a self-assertive urge weighed down by association with agression and hostility. The flood-death ending, through extreme condensation, satisfies both sides of the conflict. It brings union with Tom, which means Oedipal fulfillment, participation in masculinity, and participation in the mother's love. It also provides Maggie with an occasion to assert herself, while it brings Tom his punishment as an unloving parent-substitute. If Maggie's own death by drowning is self-punishment, it is also a kind of "oceanic bliss"—the ultimate oral fulfillment.

In *Silas Marner* the fatal condensation of *The Mill on the Floss* is avoided by separating conflicting elements. Oral-dependent needs and superego demands stand out in the Godfrey Cass plot, where they are satisfied through a "good" mother-substitute (Nancy). At the same time rage and resentment are neutralized by disposing of the "bad" brother (Dunstan) and the "bad" mother-figure (Molly). Thus the manifest love and marriage resolution veils an oral-regressive retreat from feared anal and Oedipal wishes.

The Silas story, on the other hand, moves from anal-retentive solipsism toward an Oedipal configuration (The Eppie-Silas bond) which entails reintegration and reconciliation. It can be seen as a symbolic exploration of the state of separation so intolerable for Maggie, an exploration which involves the emergence from repression of an archaic self within the author. That self, as embodied in Silas, can be reintegrated with the external world because of its *own* inherent impulse to love and also because of its separation from the past—from past injuries and resentments. Thus separation seems to be revealed (though not necessarily consciously recognized) as a potentially positive condition and point of departure.

Romola, though cramped by defensive reversals and projections, expresses the rage and resentment that were largely avoided in *Silas Marner*. Tito seeks separation from the past and from a resented, oppressive stepfather. It is the parent, Baldassare, who is abandoned and seeks vengeance. Thus rage against the "bad" parent is expressed through a crucial reversal. Romola's quest, on the other hand, presupposes the regressive needs that dominated Maggie. They are, for the most part, projected outside her. But her search for moral certainties is essentially a struggle to avoid separation and preserve a oneness or integration based on an idealized relationship to a father. That relationship is both Oedipal and oral-dependent and is rationalized (to satisfy the superego) as duty. When a succession of father-figures fail to fulfill the idealized role on which Romola's life of duty depends, the ideal of oneness with the father collapses, giving way to a separateness which is also a return to the oneness of the womb.

Through Romola's brief isolation a significant connection is made between the pain of separation and the need for maternal comfort. Although Romola finds no mother, her experience issues in a reintegration through mothering which, like Silas Marner's, satisfies oral-dependent needs vicariously. But here the manifest emphasis is defensive—mothering must be made a new duty in order to satisfy superego demands.

I have called the ending of *The Mill on the Floss* an explosive expression of conflicting needs, as powerful as a primal scream but more complex. I should emphasize here that the most basic of those needs—the one most closely associated with the primal scream—is the need for reunion with the mother. For Maggie there is essentially a blank where the mother should be. The blank suggests that the conflict responsible for Maggie's death will only become manageable when the hungry child's resentment and longing become reconnected with the missing mother. In *Silas Marner* and *Romola* the rebirths and reversals to mothering are steps toward making such a connection. Silas and Romola find children whose abandoned state tentatively exposes the author's most deeply hidden wound. Godfrey, Eppie, and Tessa actually find mother-substitutes. But these approaches are kept securely isolated from any expression of resentment or portrayal of the "bad" mother.

Felix Holt develops further these approaches to the primary separation conflict and, at the same time, begins exploring resolutions to the more advanced Oedipal conflict. The "bad" mother is objectified, at last, in Mrs. Transome, who is made to suffer the pain of isolation and loss of love. The "terrible vision" of her suffering concludes Esther's recovery of the past, freeing her to move out of her family-romance daydreams into a marriage that draws together genital, pre-genital, and moral concerns. The mother-confrontation usurps the initial emphasis placed on the titular hero's transformation of anal rage into reforming zeal. When Felix Holt's defensive response to Oedipal disillusionment becomes unmanageable, it is transferred to the non-heroic Harold Transome, whose confrontation with his father parallels that of Esther with Mrs. Transome.

The "good" characters in *Felix Holt* (Felix and Rufus Lyon) are dominated by superego demands. Their fears, and the limitations resulting from their defenses a-gainst instinctual impulses, are indirectly revealed and then anxiously concealed. In *Middlemarch*, however, these tentative explorations are expanded, and the characters governed by superego demands are not spared. In manifold ways the cost of self-hate and the "search for glory," of repression, guilt, and narcissistic illusion, is counted. The "small hungry shivering self" of the author, confronted in many ways since *The Mill on the Floss*, finds its complete negative embodiment in Casaubon's hidden death-in-life. At the same time the longings, fears, resentments, and "shoulds" of Maggie are recast in Dorothea and "worked through"—beyond self-denial, despair, and death.

We can see that the regressive needs and defenses submerged in these novels are characteristic of the depressive personality. Psychoanalysis postulates that for some individuals even the "usual and unavoidable disappointments" of childhood—"the birth of siblings, experiences of minor humiliations, penis envy, or the frustrations of the Oedipus longings"—may be narcissistic injuries severe enough to cause a "primary depression" which becomes a prototype for later reactions to frustration and loss. More often, however, a person predisposed to severe depression has suffered narcissistic injuries in his relationship with both parents at an age when self-esteem depended upon a sharing of the parent's omnipotence.[1]

In either case the personality that develops is dominated by oral-dependency in terms of requiring external supplies for the maintenance of self-esteem, and thus abhors separation or loss of love above all things. Conflict enters not only because the exaggerated need, originating in injury or loss, is built upon repressed resentment (which threatens to emerge whenever love

[1] Otto Fenichel, *The Psychoanalytic Theory of Neurosis* (New York, 1945), pp. 404-5.

objects fail to grant the reassurance that is needed), but also because individuality—even life itself—demands separation.

We do not need to locate a "primary depression" in Marian Evans's childhood in order to connect the depressions we read of in her letters to early frustrations. The separation she experienced at the age of five was undoubtedly important. Sent away to boarding school because of her mother's ill health, she suffered intensely from fear of the dark and from cold. But an earlier crisis at home when she was two years old, the birth and death of twin boys, was probably of greater significance in relation to conflicts involving the mother, self-esteem, guilt, and a sadistic superego.

Our understanding of Marian Evans as a person can be augmented by careful consideration of the latent material we find in the novels. And this can be done without reducing her greatness to a list of neurotic aims. For instance, we can see the social isolation resulting from her unsanctioned union with George Henry Lewes as more than an historical misfortune. Many of George Eliot's deepest needs were met by Lewes. She could undoubtedly identify with him as an unattractive, rejected, sickly, and still creative person. He needed her mothering and encouragement as much as she needed his. In addition it is also probable that she unconsciously needed the rejection and separation that resulted from her alliance with him. In one sense that rejection provided an opportunity for mastering the early childhood rejection. In another sense, because it blocked any ongoing relationship to her family and her past, the separation made it possible and even urgent for her to create. She was already a writer. Now she could rework the origins from which she felt cut off.

It might be interesting to explore more fully the relationship between the regressive needs expressed in the novels and the crucial events of George Eliot's life. But the question that interests me most, and the one I would like to leave in the mind of the reader, concerns the relationship between those needs and the creative process.

Part of George Eliot's motivation to create comes undeniably from the pressure of the regressive needs we have been discussing. But what about the confrontation and positive progression we have witnessed? Psychoanalytic theory is more fully developed in its comprehension of the malfunctioning psyche than in its understanding of the "normal" or the "creative." And this limitation becomes a danger if we allow our ability to uncover unconscious needs and their disguises to become an exclusive or reductive process.

I have tried to overcome this danger by showing how the author's involvement in a character or situation can be both a regression and a confrontation, rather than one or the other. In the foregoing analysis of Dorothea's "urge to rescue" (pp. 166-168 above), for example, I analyzed the rescuing as a derivative of oral and Oedipal wishes, and as a moral ideal emerging from the negative pattern of depression or "melancholia" (Oedipal disappointment, depression, and self-reproach). This interpretation and others like it may seem reductive. The emphasis placed on the nobility of Dorothea's self-subduing acts does reveal the author's intense participation in the regressive wishes and defensive needs projected onto her heroine.

But what George Eliot accomplishes here is much

more complex and significant than disguised self-expression or self-deception. Her treatment of Dorothea can be seen as a kind of self-analysis in which there is a splitting of the ego such as that described by Fenichel as part of the psychoanalytic process.

In analysis the "reasonable judging portion" of the ego observes the "experiencing portion" (which is involved in some "derivative behavior"), recognizing the latter "as not appropriate in the present and as coming from the past."[2] There is a parallel, I think, in the creative process. Whereas in analysis the patient's derivative behavior is mirrored by the analyst (who interprets without responding emotionally) in George Eliot's situation the derivative behavior is mirrored for her "reasonable" ego by the created character. The experiencing portion of the author's ego is deeply involved in the regressive behavior of the character. But that character also becomes an objectification or mirror confronting the non-regressive aspect of the author's ego.

The parallel is not exact, of course, but the analytic terms can help us to understand how both regression and confrontation are involved, and how George Eliot finds in the creation of Dorothea a new resolution for the dilemma that ended in the death of Maggie.

[2] Ibid., p. 570. This activity involves what Heinz Hartmann calls a "transvaluation of moral values" (in *Psychoanalysis and Moral Values*, New York, 1960, pp. 30-31): "On the long way from the interiorization of parental demands after the Oedipal conflicts to the more elaborate moral codes of the adult another factor becomes decisive. That is a process of generalization, or formalization, and of integration of moral values. It would be difficult to attribute what I have in mind here to the superego itself. It rather corresponds to what we know of the functions of the ego.

To deny this would be to concur with Calvin Bedient that for George Eliot "all sacrifice is for the best," and that her distinction lies simply in "coloring and shaping" Victorian morality—"the aberration of an age."[3] What Bedient fails to see is that in *Middlemarch* and in all the works leading up to it, the author is struggling with her Victorian idea of the self, testing it, changing it, and transcending it. Self-denial, as an aspect of the activity of the sadistic superego, is a single component of a conflict between the desire to maintain a relationship to a love object and the desire to punish (even destroy) that object for its incapacity to satisfy one's needs. But Bedient does not seem to be aware that there is any conflict, let alone that George Eliot has the ego-strength to work it through to a self-affirming resolution.

It is not, as Bedient supposes, that George Eliot's literary greatness proves to be independent of her model of the self. On the contrary, it is her exploration and testing of that model that makes *Middlemarch* possible—not "one of the miracles of art," but the creative culmination of a long process of self-confrontation.

The psychoanalytic approach can help us to avoid oversimplifications such as Bedient's. But in order to use it wisely, we must be willing to admit that the theory, as it now stands, is not capable of completely unraveling the mysteries of the creative process. Freudian psychoanalysis has gone beyond Freud in distinguishing the creative from the neurotic. Philip Rieff argues that Freud's most mature statements, though not pursued, suggest a view of art as "not merely a form of acceding

[3] *Architects of the Self* (Berkeley and Los Angeles, 1972), pp. 45-53, 81-82, 268.

to one's feelings" but as a means of achieving mastery.[4]
Whether we give Freud the credit or not, we can see a
definite development of this view among psychoanalytic
ego-psychologists. Thus Ernst Kris sees the artist as
having a "capacity of gaining easy access to id material
without being overwhelmed by it."[5] His ego regression,
unlike the neurotic's, is "partial and temporary" and
"controlled by the ego which retains the function of
establishing contact with an audience."[6]

The concept of regression in the service of the ego is
a step in the right direction. The artist is seen as flexible,
controlling rather than controlled by his regressive
impulses, and a work of art is not merely "an occasion
to contemplate the unconscious frozen into one of its
possible gestures."[7] But we are still left without concepts which really help us to understand fully the
dynamic relationship that exists between George Eliot
and her creations.[8] We have seen evidence that the
objectification of her inner conflicts changed the face of
reality for the author and contributed to the creation of

[4] *Freud: The Mind of the Moralist* (New York, 1959), p. 383.

[5] "The Contribution and Limitations of Psychoanalysis," in *Art and
Psychoanalysis,* ed. William Phillips (Cleveland, 1963), p. 283.

[6] *Psychoanalytic Explorations in Art* (New York, 1952), p. 167.

[7] Rieff, p. 134.

[8] In *The Dynamics of Creation* (New York, 1972) Anthony Storr reevaluates accepted views of ego and id functions in the light of modern
research on the creative personality. He explores the ego strengths of
the creative person, as well as the characteristic need to establish a
firmer identity. He also finds that the pattern-making function of the
mind is, to a large extent, "beyond the control of the conscious will,
and that the unconscious from which it takes origin can no longer
usefully be regarded as simply the product of repression." See
especially his chapter on "Man's Inner World: Origin and Function"
where he discusses the "old brain" and its record of early childhood
experiences (pp. 158-61).

more positive resolutions. And we cannot be true to our experience of her novels if we discount their preponderant constructiveness as merely defensive transformation of regressive fantasy.

.   .   .

Jessamyn West speaks of writing, or the life of the imagination, as a "struggle with the self." Sometimes, she says, "it is only by writing the story that the novelist can discover—not his story—but its writer."[9] By this she does not mean establishing an "angle of vision," but discovering which of the many persons necessarily within the writer is the "true voice." The discovery of the "true voice" amid "this embarrassment of persons" demands a selection, but it can paradoxically only be made through openness":

By openness I do not mean "open-mindedness" nor openness to experience"; though these states might well attend the kind of openness of which I speak. Perhaps I had better say what this openness is not. It is not self-protection. It is not hatred. It is not impatience. It is not answers. It is not facts. It is not justification. It is not pride. It is not a fist, it is not a clenching.

It is exposure. It is space. Without space, without openness, the world of the novel cannot grow. It can only be made. . . . A clenching kills. And hate, which is a clenching, which is a focusing of great narrowness, kills. . . . Openness, persisted in, destroys hate. The novelist may begin his writing with every intention of destroying what he hates. Since a novelist writes of persons this means the destruction (through revelation) of an evil person. But writing in openness, which means a becoming and not a describing or talking about, the writer becomes the evil person, does what the evil person does, for his reasons and with his justifications. As this takes place, as the novelist opens himself to evil, a self-righteous hatred of

[9] "The Slave Cast Out," in *The Living Novel,* ed. Granville Hicks (New York, 1957), pp. 201-2.

evil is no longer possible. The evil which now exists is within; and one is self-righteous in relation to others, not to one's self. Just as the man who pities is suspect unless he himself has experienced the pitiable state, or is willing to enter it if that will help, so is the novelist suspect who writes of evil without openness to evil. Now that he has himself assumed the aspects of evil and does not condemn from the outside magisterially, he can bring to his readers understanding and elicit from them compassion.[10]

This condition of "openness," as Jessamyn West points out, is perhaps what Keats calls "negative capability." It is related in my mind to the artist's ego strength and his capacity to make contact with his unconscious. And I have included it here because it captures the kind of self-confrontation and growth I have seen in George Eliot's novels and felt ill-equipped to describe. It also serves as a reminder that our criticism of literature, if it is to enhance rather than diminish our ability to participate in creative work, will probably have to resist "self-protection" and "clenching" and submit to "openness":

> The mind that is too ready at contempt
> and reprobation is . . . as a clenched
> fist that can give blows, but is shut up
> from receiving and holding ought that
> is precious—though it were heaven-
> sent manna.
>
> *Felix Holt*

[10] Ibid., pp. 202-3.

Bibliography

Allen, Walter. *George Eliot.* New York: Macmillan, 1964.

Allott, Miriam. "George Eliot in the 1860's." *Victorian Studies* 5 (December 1961): 94-109.

Armstrong, Isobel. *"Middlemarch:* A Note on George Eliot's 'Wisdom.' " In *Critical Essays on George Eliot* (see Hardy).

Bedient, Calvin. *Architects of the Self: George Eliot, D. H. Lawrence, and E. M. Forster.* Berkeley and Los Angeles: University of California Press, 1972.

Bennett, Joan. *George Eliot: Her Mind and Her Art.* Cambridge: At the University Press, 1948.

Bethell, S. L. "The Novels of George Eliot." *The Criterion* 17 (October 1938-January 1939):39-57.

Bonaparte, Marie. *Female Sexuality.* New York: International Universities Press, 1953.

Bourl'honne, P. *George Eliot: Essai de biographie intellectuelle et morale, 1819-1854.* Paris, HMS Presse, 1933.

Brenner, Charles. *An Elementary Textbook of Psychoanalysis.* New York: Doubleday Anchor Books, 1957.

Bullett, Gerald. *George Eliot: Her Life and Books.* New Haven: Yale University Press, 1948.

Bush, Marshall. "The Problem of Form in the Psychoanalytic Theory of Art." *Psychoanalytic Review* 54 (1967): 5-35.

Carroll, David R., "An Image of Disenchantment in the Novels of George Eliot." *Review of English Studies* 11 (1960): 29-41.

————. *"Felix Holt:* Society as Protagonist." *Nineteenth-Century Fiction* 17 (1962-63):237-53.

————. *"Silas Marner:* Reversing the Oracles of Religion." In *Literary Monographs,* I, edited by Eric Rothstein and Thomas K. Dunseath. Madison: University of Wisconsin Press, 1967.

————, ed. *George Eliot: The Critical Heritage*. New York: Barnes and Noble, 1971.

Cecil, David. *Early Victorian Novelists*. London, 1934; reprinted (as *Victorian Novelists*), Chicago: University of Chicago Press, 1958.

Cooley, E. Mason. "Uses of Melodrama in George Eliot's Fiction." Ph.D. dissertation, University of California, Berkeley, 1962.

Copland, Aaron. *Music and Imagination*. Cambridge, Mass.: Harvard University Press, 1952.

Crews, Frederick. "Anaesthetic Criticism." In *Psychoanalysis and Literary Process*, edited by Frederick Crews. Cambridge, Mass.: Winthrop Publishers, 1970.

Crompton, Margaret. *George Eliot, the Woman*. New York: Yoseloff, 1960.

Deutsch, Helene. *The Psychology of Women*. 2 vols. New York: Grune, 1944.

Eliot, George (Marian Evans). *Felix Holt, the Radical*. Warwickshire Edition. 2 vols. New York, 1907.

————. *Middlemarch*. Edited by Gordon S. Haight. Riverside Edition. Boston: Houghton Mifflin, 1956.

————. *The Mill on the Floss*. Edited by Gordon S. Haight. Riverside Edition. Boston: Houghton Mifflin, 1961.

————. *Romola*. Warwickshire Edition. 2 vols. New York, 1907.

————. *Silas Marner*. New York: Holt, Rinehart and Winston, 1962.

Erikson, Erik H. *Childhood and Society*. New York: Norton, 1960.

————. *Identity: Youth and Crisis*. New York: Norton, 1968.

Fenichel, Otto. *The Psychoanalytic Theory of Neurosis*. New York: Norton, 1945.

Fliess, Robert, ed. *The Psychoanalytic Reader: An Anthology of Essential Papers*. New York: International Universities Press, 1948.

Freud, Sigmund. *The Standard Edition of the Complete Psychological Works of Sigmund Freud*, edited by James Strachey. 24 vols. London: Hogarth Press, 1953-74.

Greenacre, Phyllis. *The Quest for the Father*. New York: International Universities Press, 1963.

Haddakin, Lilian. "*Silas Marner*." In *Critical Essays on George Eliot* (see Hardy).

Haight, Gordon S. *George Eliot: A Biography*. New York and Oxford: Oxford University Press, 1968.

————. *George Eliot and John Chapman*. New Haven: Yale University Press, 1940.

————, ed. *A Century of George Eliot Criticism*. Boston: Houghton Mifflin, 1965.
————. *The George Eliot Letters*. 7 vols. New Haven: Yale University Press, 1954-55.
Hardy, Barbara. *The Appropriate Form*. London: Northwestern University Press, 1964.
————. *The Novels of George Eliot: A Study in Form*. London: Athlone Press, 1959.
————, ed. *Critical Essays on George Eliot*. New York: Barnes and Noble, 1970.
————. *"Middlemarch": Critical Approaches to the Novel*. New York: Oxford University Press, 1967.
Hartmann, Heinz. *Psychoanalysis and Moral Values*. New York: International Universities Press, 1960.
Harvey, W. J. *The Art of George Eliot*. London: Oxford University Press, 1961.
————. "George Eliot." In *Victorian Fiction: A Guide to Research* (see Stevenson).
————. "Idea and Image in the Novels of George Eliot." In *Critical Essays on George Eliot* (see Hardy).
Holland, Norman N. *The Dynamics of Literary Response*. New York: Oxford University Press, 1968.
————. "Freud and the Poet's Eye." In *Hidden Patterns: Studies in Psychoanalytic Literary Criticism*, edited by Leonard Manheim and Eleanor Manheim. New York: Macmillan, 1966.
————. "Reply: Dynamics Revisted." *Literature and Psychology* 21, no. 1 (1971): 59-62.
————. "Why Organic Unity." *College English* 30 (1968): 19-30.
Holmstrom, John, and Lerner, Laurence, eds. *George Eliot and Her Readers*. New York: Barnes and Noble, 1966.
Horney, Karen. *Neurosis and Human Growth*. New York: Norton, 1950.
James, Henry. "George Eliot's *Middlemarch*." *Galaxy* 15 (March 1873): 424-38; reprinted in *A Century of George Eliot Criticism* (see Haight).
Jones, R. T. *George Eliot*. Cambridge: At the University Press, 1970.
Kettle, Arnold. *"Felix Holt, the Radical."* In *Critical Essays on George Eliot* (see Hardy).
Knoepflmacher, U. C. *George Eliot's Early Novels: The Limits of Realism*. Berkeley and Los Angeles: University of California Press, 1968.
————. *Laughter and Despair: Readings in the Novels of the Victorian*

Era. Berkeley and Los Angeles: University of California Press, 1971.

————. *Religious Humanism and the Victorian Novel*. Princeton: Princeton University Press, 1965.

Koenigsberg, Richard A. "Culture and Unconscious Fantasy: Observations on Courtly Love." *Psychoanalytic Review* 54 (1967): 36-49.

Kris, Ernst. "The Contributions and Limitations of Psychoanalysis." In *Art and Psychoanalysis* (see Phillips).

————. *Psychoanalytic Explorations in Art*. New York: International Universities Press, 1952.

Kroeber, Karl. *Styles in Fictional Structure: The Art of Jane Austen, Charlotte Bronte, George Eliot*. Princeton: Princeton University Press, 1971.

Langer, Suzanne K. *Philosophy in a New Key*. New York: Mentor, 1951.

Leavis, F. R. *The Great Tradition*. New York: New York University Press, 1964.

Lerner, Lawrence. *The Truthtellers: Jane Austen, George Eliot, and D. H. Lawrence*. New York: Schocken, 1967.

Lesser, Simon O. *Fiction and the Unconscious*. New York: Vintage Books, 1957.

Levine, George. "Intelligence as Deception: *The Mill on the Floss*." *PLMA* 80 (1965): 402-9.

————. "*Romola* as Fable." In *Critical Essays on George Eliot* (see Hardy).

McKenzie, K. A. *Edith Simcox and George Eliot*. London: Oxford University Press, 1961.

Milner, Ian. *The Structure of Values in George Eliot*. Prague: Universita Karlova, 1968.

Oldfield, Derek. "The Language of the Novel." In *"Middlemarch": Critical Approaches to the Novel* (see Hardy).

Paris, Bernard J. *Experiments in Life: George Eliot's Quest for Values*. Detroit: Wayne State University Press, 1965.

————. "The Inner Conflicts of Maggie Tulliver: A Horneyan Analysis." *Centennial Review* 13 (Spring 1969): 166-99.

Phillips, William, ed. *Art and Psychoanalysis*. Cleveland: World Publishing Company, Meridian Books, 1963.

Pine, Fred. "On the Structuralization of Drive-Defense Relationships." *Psychoanalytic Quarterly* 39 (1970): 17-37.

Rank, Otto. *The Myth of the Birth of the Hero: A Psychological Interpretation of Mythology*. Translated by R. Robbins and Smith Ely Jelliffe. New York: Brunner, 1952.

Rieff, Philip. *Freud: The Mind of the Moralist.* New York: Viking, 1959.

Robinson, Carole. *"Romola:* A Reading of the Novel." *Victorian Studies* (September 1962): 29-42.

Schorer, Mark. "The Structure of the Novel." In *"Middlemarch": Critical Approaches to the Novel* (see Hardy).

Slochower, Harry. "The Psychoanalytic Approach to Literature: Some Pitfalls and Promises," *Literature and Psychology* 21, no. 2 (1971): 107-12.

Smith, David. " 'In their death they were not divided': The Form of Illicit Passion in *The Mill on the Floss.*" *Literature and Psychology* 15, no. 3 (1965):144-62.

Speaight, Robert. *George Eliot.* New York: Roy, 1952.

Stang, Richard, ed. *Discussions of George Eliot.* Boston: Heath, 1960.

Steinhoff, William R. "Intent and Fulfillment in the Ending of *The Mill on the Floss.*" In *The Image of the Work,* edited by Bertrand Evans, Josephine Miles, and William R. Steinhoff, Berkeley and Los Angeles: University of California Press, 1955.

————. "Recurrent Patterns in George Eliot's Novels." Ph.D. dissertation, University of California, Berkeley, 1948.

Stephen, Leslie. *George Eliot.* London, 1902.

Stevenson, Lionel, ed. *Victorian Fiction: A Guide to Research.* Cambridge, Mass.: Harvard University Press, 1964.

Storr, Anthony. *The Dynamics of Creation.* New York: Atheneum, 1972.

Stump, Reva. *Movement and Vision in George Eliot's Novels.* Seattle: University of Washington Press, 1959.

Thale, Jerome. "George Eliot's Fable for Her Times." *College English* 19 (1958):141-46.

————. *The Novels of George Eliot.* New York and London: Columbia University Press, 1959.

Thomson, Fred C. "The Genesis of *Felix Holt.*" *PMLA* 74 (1959): 576-84.

Waelder, Robert. "The Principle of Multiple Function: Obervations on Over-Determination." *Psychoanalytic Quarterly* 5 (1936): 45-62.

West, Jessamyn. "The Slave Cast Out." In *The Living Novel,* edited by Granville Hicks. New York: Macmillan, 1957.

Wiesenfarth, Joseph. "Demythologizing *Silas Marner,*" *English Literary History* 37 (1970): 226-44.